CHEAP LAFFS

LOOKS LIKE A REAL BOOK!

CHEAP LAFFS

The Art of the Novelty Item

By **MARK NEWGARDEN** and **PICTUREBOX**, Inc.

Photography by MICHAEL SCHMELLING

HARRY N. ABRAMS, Inc., **PUBLISHERS**

SEE! (A REAL BOOK!)

Cheap Laffs
The Art of the Novelty Item
Mark Newgarden and
PictureBox, Inc.
Harry N. Abrams, Inc., Publishers

Written by Mark Newgarden
Edited by PictureBox, Inc. and
Mark Newgarden (assistant: Jessi Rymill)
Copy edited by Sarah Larson
Designed by PictureBox, Inc. (assistant: Lindsay Ballant)
Photography by Michael Schmelling

For Harry N. Abrams:
Project Manager: Deborah Aaronson
Production Managers: Stan Redfern and
Norman Watkins

Library of Congress Cataloging-in-Publication Data

Newgarden, Mark.
Cheap laffs : the art of the novelty item /
Mark Newgarden and PictureBox, Inc.
p. cm.
Includes bibliographical references and index.
ISBN 0-8109-5599-7
1. Novelties. I. PictureBox, Inc. II. Title.

TS2301.N55 N49 2004
688.7'26—dc22

2004006833

Printed and bound in China

10 9 8 7 6 5 4 3 2 1

Harry N. Abrams, Inc.
100 Fifth Avenue
New York, N.Y. 10011
www.abramsbooks.com

Abrams is a subsidiary of

LA MARTINIÈRE
GROUPE

THERE WAS A MAN WHO WENT TO A BAR AND EVERY NIGHT HE'D FALL ASLEEP AT THE BAR. THE BAR OWNER DIDN'T LIKE HIM AT ALL. SO ONE TIME WHEN HE WAS PASSED OUT, THE BAR-TENDER SLIPPED ONE OF THOSE FAKE VOMITS UNDER HIM. THE MAN WOKE UP—HE WASN'T DISTURBED AT ALL, APPARENTLY—HE LEFT A BIG TIP. THAT WAS THE LAST THEY SAW OF HIM.

—JOSEPH (BUD) ADAMS, 1993

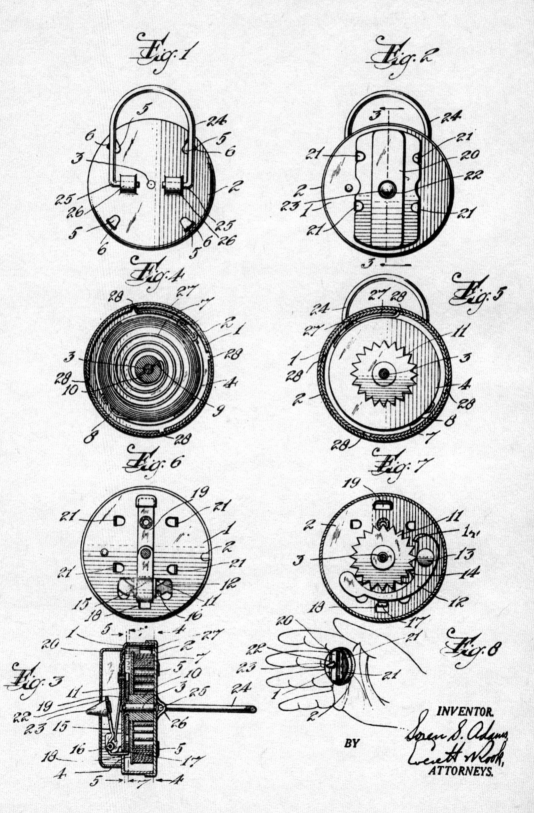

INVENTOR.

Soren S. Adams

Everett H. Rook,

BY

ATTORNEYS.

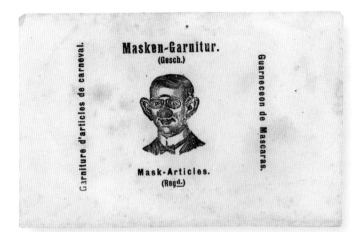

LAFF HISTORY:

AN INTRODUCTION

gags, pranks, jokes, snares, knickknacks, gimmicks, mascots, rib-ticklers, and joy-makers, laff producers, and fun-inducers: to the uninitiated, these terms ring of slangy hucksterism, yet they accurately reflect highly technical classifications of a once thriving, if marginal, industry devoted to the creation of a modest product of questionable quality, taste, originality, and necessity, targeted for fleeting high-impact diversion and doomed to remorseless disposal. Given these parameters, the novelty item shares direct kinship with all the truly significant art forms of the twentieth century.

The Joy Buzzer, The Whoopee Cushion, The Smoking Monkey. The Dying Pig. The Enormous Vibrating Eye. Fake rubber puke, snot, shit, worms, chickens, eggs, butter, nails, pencils, cigarette ashes, and pecans. What these goodies and thousands more share is a joyous, unabashedly base attempt at giving shape, substance, and shelf life to the dark, primal, uncensored roots of all that we politely like to call "humor."

Aesthetically we can only marvel at the outlandish beauty of these objects, seemingly concocted in a frenzied atmosphere of pop-cultural temperature-taking

(opposite) Original patent drawings for the Joy Buzzer, as submitted to the U.S. Patent Office by S. S. Adams in 1931.

(above) Chromolithograph paper-face kit, made in Germany, c. 1900. Packets like these were sold cheaply and with much hyperbole by Johnson Smith & Co. as well as other merchants of the day.

and reckless dementia. How else do we even begin to divine The Phony Hypo, the "Hello Sweetheart! I'm The Talking Wolf!" The Royal Flush toilet seat cover, The Little Sick Squirt, or Psycho-Ceramics? Blissfully unimpaired by proper, let alone progressive, design expectations, the look of the lowly novelty, its packaging and advertising, shared an honest, unreflexive vernacular with the tangiest dregs of twentieth-century graphics: the blunt, manic, get-happy, yet infinitely personal pen stroke of the comic strip; the flashy, gaffed exotica of the carnival banner; the informational austerity of the hand-lettered show-card; and the crude, semi-public cryptography of the tattoo image. The only design objective for the novelty was to divert, enthrall, sell the product now, and quit while you were ahead. It's hard to imagine a better petri dish for potential greatness.

Perhaps the defining feature of these inglorious articles is their essential, unapologetic utilitarianism. They were certainly not conceived as Art for its own aesthetic sake. Neither were they truly intended as toys, crafted with any deliberate "play value" or "eye appeal" to charm an indulgent parent. These items were designed to appeal to the child-like and the child-ish, if not necessarily the child himself. They were, above all, consumer product—manufactured with a profit incentive and a live-or-die verdict from an audience who purchased them directly, if surreptitiously, for its own unspoken motives. This unequivocal customer base was the *user*; and these were objects precision-made to be used with one goal in mind—the production

Imitation Fly Pin
JAPAN

of laughter (and the inevitable byproducts of pain and suffering that always lurk in its shadow). Form never followed function more ruthlessly than in the joke dinner roll made of solid rock.

Market research came via the school of hard knocks, gathered strictly by the seat of the pants and the gurgle of the gut of those anonymous men whose livelihoods depended upon an item's ability to deliver the yucks (and the orders) again and again. As gag maven Sam Oumano explained in 1965:

I've been on the road seventeen years, and I've had people tell me they wouldn't buy a gag because they know plenty of practical jokes. They're the real sadist types who let the air out of your tires so you drive off a cliff. Why nail a guy's shoes to the floor when you could do better to buy something original? Our canned gags are only a beginning. The build-up takes imagination, real acting talent. Take our imitation doorknob and our imitation faucet that sticks on any kind of wall by suction.[i] A fellow with imagination can turn these into real good jokes. We had a man in Teaneck who started a little fire in a wastebasket and yelled for water. His party guests all made a jump for the faucet. Half the living room burned up. You see, you have to handle the joke right to get the most out of it.[ii]

But Oumano and his brethren were not merely providing the stage props for real-life "acting out." The best and longest lasting of these products achieved an iconic status that transcended any inherent novelty value.

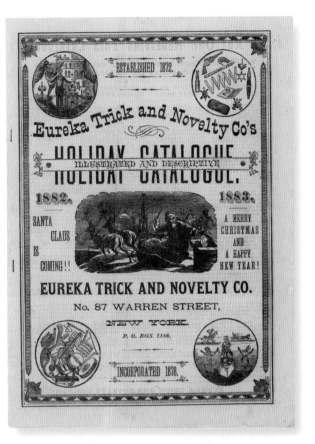

These became the industry staples, sacramental American objects· that were purchased again and again for each successive generation's ritual use, because, at the bottom line, they simply worked.

Much of their origin remains forever lost. These are not the histories of our nation's greatness handed down in high-school textbooks. "Who created fake dog doo? I don't know who. How far do dogs go back? When was the dog invented?" deadpanned second-generation prankman Joseph (Bud) Adams of the S. S. Adams Co.[iii] There are simply no extant records from the dawn of the industrial revolution on the production runs of faux bedbugs, but simple dolls were commercially fabricated in Nuremburg, Germany ("The Birthplace of Technology"), on a cottage-industry basis as early as the fourteenth century and from there a great international industry blossomed. In 1798, one Nuremberg department store listed no fewer than eight thousand individual items in its toy catalog alone, all fabricated in that increasingly powerful center of trade.[iv] By the nineteenth century, industrial-revolution–era Germany was known as "Toy Maker to the World"—but industrial-revolution–era Germany was known also, without particularly trying very hard, as the world's premier party-favor maker, magic-kit maker, imitation-spider maker, false-whisker maker, rubber-tongue maker, surprise-cigar maker, agitating-cheese maker, and squirting-ring maker as well.

In the United States, large urban department stores handled the earliest transactions of these "gross" imports, and traveling salesmen carried them west via the covered wagon and the rails in our nation's great expansion. Chain stores and mail-order empires founded by the shrewdest of these hucksters realized in the novelty item an ideal product—new, cheap, small, easy to ship, easy to store, and infinitely desirable. The Eureka Trick And Novelty Co. was established in lower Manhattan in 1872, and with its emphasis on "trick" was certainly among the earliest emporiums of its kind. As noted in the August 1877 edition of *Cricket on the Hearth:*

Persons wanting Tricks, Games or Novelties will find The Eureka Trick And Novelty Co. a prompt, low-priced and efficient firm to deal with. This is an old-established house, well known & reliable and one to whom we give a hearty recommendation.

The self-described "importers, manufacturers, wholesale and retail dealers" occupied a four-thousand—square-foot store at 87 Warren Street, and issued their initial mail-order catalog for Christmas, 1882, approximately a full third of which could reasonably be described as "tricks."

The domestic toy industry in America had expanded exponentially since the 1830s. An 1850 U.S. census listed forty-seven dedicated toy makers,[v] and certainly some of the increasingly diverse wares of these Yankee inventors could likely be classified under the always somewhat blurry designation of "novelties." One surviving 1875 mail-order catalog of U.S.-patented and domestically made articles was issued by the Inventors Union at 173 Greenwich Street, New York City, and included along with such mundane household hardware such as The Little Giant Tack Hammer and Aunt Peggy's Rasp Corn Killer, several amateur magicians' card illusions; The (squirting) Finger Ring Trick; Comic White Rubber Elastic Heads; and The Mysterious Magic Finger ("Oh Mother Look at Papa's Finger through the Crown of his Hat").

Hundreds more of these off-the-cuff entrepreneurs, whether inventing, fabricating, or importing their wares, sprung into action to live out the American dream by catering to a growing demand for the increasing variety of these newfangled personal-entertainment devices whose blunt, primal appeal cut directly across all ethnic, language, class, age, and seasonal lines.

But it was not until the booming years of the early twentieth century that the cheap-

laff industry truly came of age in America, with the inventions and enterprise of one prank-loving young Danish immigrant whose legacy has come to structure our understanding of these ephemeral objects and their place in our culture. In 1906, a young, fast-talking, champion sharpshooter and freshly retired coal-tar—dye salesman named Soren (Sam) Sorenson set himself up in a one-room office in Plainfield, New Jersey, and proceeded to spend his days funneling a powdered derivative of an imported German coal tar into small bottles affixed with labels bearing the word "Cachoo."

He had taken quick notice (and some pleasure) in his former dye company coworkers' spontaneous sneezing fits when exposed to the pernicious gray dust, and he began to

w India rubber toys made to blow up, high class finished articles.

No. 1720. **Flying sausages.** Per Gross 6/6, 10 Gross 60/—.

No. 2087. **The dying turk.** Per Gross 48/—.

No. 2086. **The "Homunculus" or "the missing link" or Mankind in 1000 years.** Per Gross 48/—.

1852. **Dying Stork.** Per Gross 39/—.

No. 1853. **Dying Chauffeur.** Per Gross 60/—.

No. 1666. **Dying Iky.** Per Gross 21/—.

No. 968. **Bi, Bi.** Well known article with voice. Per Gross 6/6. In 10 Gross lots 60/—. No. 96/1. Small sort per Gross 3/3, 10 Gross 30/—.

est novelty ::: **Apparatus to fill "Indiarubber-air-balloons" with gas.**
With description for use per Doz. Apparatus 36/— or 3/— a piece.
Indiarubber-air-balloons first quality rubber.
d 40 cm circumference Gross 8/—, 100 Gross 600/—.   **Round 50 cm** circumference Gross 10/—, 100 Gross 850/—.
Advertising print for 1 Gross 1 3, for 10 Gross 10/—, for 50 Gross 30/— extra.
eppeliniform, 40 cm long Gross 21/—, 60 cm long 38 — per Gross. Advertising print 2 6 per Gross extra.
— 1 —

My Dumb Traveler, manufacturer's wholesale novelty catalog. N. L. Chrestensen, Erfurt, Germany, 1910.

and a forty-thousand–square-foot–long factory on the Jersey shore, fully equipped to tear-bomb a laff-happy public with hundreds more manufactured hilarities via boxcar. Sam's success formula was elementary: "The whole basic idea of a good joke novelty is that it has to be simple and easy to work…The reaction should always be unexpected."[vi] On February 10, 1948, the corporation issued a press release noting the sale of its millionth vial of Cachoo. Adams became known as "the Henry Ford of fun."

Prank-meisters proliferated. Anyone with a small bankroll and a big idea could grab a stake in the "boffs for bucks" gold rush. Hundreds, if not thousands, more retailers, catalog houses, salesmen, jobbers, middlemen, wholesalers, importers, manufacturers, inventors, and ambidextrous combos of any of the above exploded onto the scene, all creatively riffing upon (or outright stealing) each other's surefire million-dollar ideas.

Sam Oumano, a well-educated Sephardic Jew fresh off the boat from Turkey and its newest persecutory regime, peddled Indian moccasins and picture postcards from a pushcart on the streets of Manhattan at the turn of the century.[vii] In 1909, a year when the fledgling novelty industry grossed a mere $100,000,[viii] Sam, with the backing of his brothers Dave and Eli, launched a souvenir and joke shop at 1209 Broadway, in the city's latest theater district. The Franco-American Novelty Co. (Sam spoke French fluently and had taught it in the old country) was born, eventually expanding into piecework production from the Oumano family's West Bronx kitchen table while continuing to import and

carry small quantities on his person for his own extemporaneous off-duty jollies. People sneezed; then laughed; then asked for a bottle. Sam bet his bankroll that a whole lot more folks would get the same charge out of introducing the irritating industrial residue to their friends too, and within one year he had reportedly sold 150,000 bottles at a dime each. Sam never looked back. Living the dream large, he Americanized his name to Samuel Sorenson Adams and in the next few years followed up his Cachoo windfall with The Bingo Shooter—a miniature mousetrap that shot percussive caps—then The Rocket Wireless Message (today known as Rattlesnake Eggs), The Fake Ink Blot, The Funny Dribble Glass, Snake Surprise Cans, the Joy Buzzer, and eventually forty patents

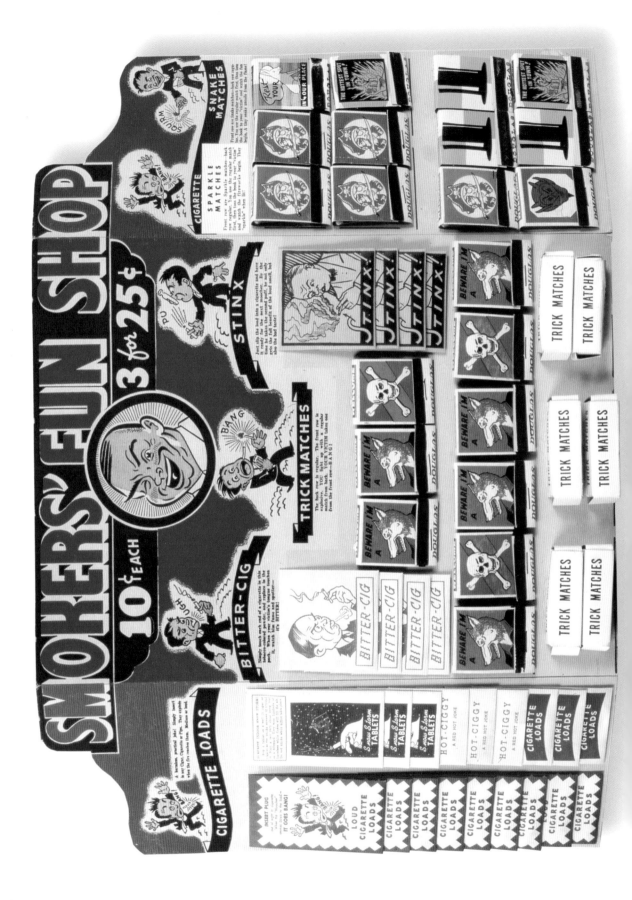

retail a line of sundry amusements. Franco-American boldly pioneered, if it did not technically author, such transcendental humorists' tools as The Jumping Snake Can, The Poo Poo Raspberry Cushion, and fake dog stool ("Dogonnit" brand). "If you didn't find something to laugh at you'd die. People need laughter," declared the sage entrepreneur, whose hand-to-mouth enterprise had become the world's largest novelty distributor by the mid-1960s.[ix] "Franco created the joke and trick industry," maintains industry elder statesman (and longtime Franco salesman) Sol Pritt. "I would say the Franco items were more everlasting. Timeless. Dog shit, the cans, those items live on and on."[x]

The Richard Appel Co. of New York had its roots in one of the largest novelty houses in Nuremburg, Germany, going back to the nineteenth century. Appel, a German Jew, fled his native country sometime in the 1930s, apparently losing his business directly to Alfred Rosenberg, the notorious Nazi Reich Minister. Under Hitler's personal orders, Rosenberg headed an infamous unit known as Einsatzstab Rosenberg, which plundered Jewish libraries, institutions, and objects of art throughout occupied western Europe. Rosenberg, who was also reportedly something of "a jokester,"[xi] was later found guilty at Nuremberg on four counts of war crimes and crimes against humanity, and was sentenced to death by hanging. By 1941, Richard Appel had established his signature Jo King product line in America, distinguished in its packaging by a grinning little bean-headed mascot of the same name. He was at that time considered to be Adams's closest rival, though "no tycoon yet,"[xii] and

has been credited with giving the world The Backfiring Carving Knife, The Dud Fire Cracker, and spoons that melt in your mouth.[xiii] The Jo King brand found its true niche, however, with a lowdown assortment of sparkling, shooting, and exploding items, persisting with the treacherous Smokers Fun type of in-your-face fireworks, long after Adams and the others had judiciously dropped such risky offerings. "Not really funny, but a nice person,"[xiv] Richard Appel, the "progressive, scrappy and fast on his feet"[xv] survivor, apparently hung onto the cheap-laff business well into the 1950s.

Hyman (Chaim) Fishlov was a printer and bookseller who chanced to vacation abroad in July, 1914, and was quickly persuaded that the climate for Jewish businessmen in America was much healthier than in his native Ukraine.[xvi] He settled in Chicago and began his adventures in retail by hawking cast-metal toy soldiers door to door. Eventually established as H. Fishlove & Co., his small toy and novelty business prospered. From the 1920s onward, under the creative leadership of son Irving, the enterprise expanded into the manufacturing end, specializing in risqué, double-entendre, fake-out gift packages known industry-wide as "Box Gags" (a small box scientifically labeled "World's Smallest Receiving Set" opens to reveal a miniature metal commode). The company hit real pay dirt in the 1930s and '40s with one called Tricky Dogs: boxed, twin black-and-white plastic Scotties, eternally inspecting each other's derrières via polarized magnets mounted underneath their bases. The Scotties became the company's all-time bestseller and easily one of the most

(opposite) H. Fishlove & Co. celebrates
and sings itself in this 1960s sales sheet
for the Giant Specs series of novelties.

ubiquitous manufactured ephemeral products of the twentieth century.[xvii] The
Fishlove brain trust always kept a dutiful
pulse on the specialized needs of the toilet-
and-body–humor connoisseur, eventually
creating some of the most iconoclastic and
fabulously surreal objects in the marketplace,
like the Yakity-Yak Talking Teeth (courtesy
the pop-creative smarts of the legendary toy-
design company Marvin Glass & Associates),
The Phony Faucet, and Mr. John, the faux-
ceramic, full-size portable urinal.

While these and other companies in this
small, somewhat incestuous industry co-
existed on more-or-less friendly terms ("like
family—with all the dysfunctionality that
goes along with it,")[xviii] the most problemat-
ic competition came from overseas, where
labor was cheap and hard-won patents were,
as often as not, just considered another joke.

Adams recalled in 1946: "I invented a
glass which leaks, the famous Dribble Glass
which is probably the most pirated item I
ever had. Although I got a patent on it the
Japs and the Germans and the fly-by-nights
in this country drove me crazy with their
cheap imitations of it, and they undersold
me by fifty percent."[xix] With every new successful item came the inevitable circling buz-
zards of quick-buck clones and retroactive
"creators." Cachoo was reportedly pirated
within two months.[xx] The incentive was
strong enough—Adams enjoyed an average
mark-up of 150 percent on his items.[xxi]
Without the resources to legally enjoin each
slippery knock-off artist (nor the particular
incentive to protect an ephemeral item that
might not sell past next Tuesday anyway), the
furtive industrialists became even more guard-

ed as to their stock's origins and originality.

Sol Pritt, then a rookie joke broker,
recalled: "After World War II, when I was
discharged, I got involved with jokes and
tricks. My father was a great gagster. He had
a company manufacturing military insignia,
and he was in the jewelry business, and he
knocked off Fishlove. Fishlove had those
Tricky Dogs, and Dad said, 'I like that item.
I'm gonna knock it off.' I said, 'Dad, Fishlove
owns it.' He said, 'I don't care, I want it.'"[xxii]
Nostalgic veterans warmly recall one golden
moment of prosperity when twenty-five
individual manufacturers competed for the
lucrative man-made–dog-feces market.
Savvy industry analysts were said to be able
to accurately determine which breed of dog
a retailer owned based on that retailer's professional assessment of product realism.[xxiii]

Ultimately, the true survivors clenched
their Goofy Teeth, resigned themselves to
the hard facts of the glee peddler's trade, and
moved on to the next big monkeyshine. In
1965, Sam Oumano was still boasting of his
firm's countermeasures to thwart the copy-
cats: "We have hidden factories, top security.
You couldn't go in there if you tried."[xxiv] But
it was late in the game, and by the post-
World War II era, an ever-increasing bulk of
product in the marketplace was a new type of
import: cheaper-still versions of the cheap-
laff originals, flashily carded for mass-mar-
ket display, labeled "Made in Japan" and,
eventually, "Taiwan." When the Joy Buzzer's
patents ran out in 1960, the market was
flooded by rattletrap Japanese forgeries. For a
time, unable to compete financially, the S. S.
Adams Company was economically forced to
fill its yearly orders of some 150,000 units

The original and best made
Giant Specs
Distortion-free lenses! Attractive Packages That Sell!

Comical! Astonishing!
HOLLYWOOD
SUPER-SPECS
Largest, funniest glasses ever made!

The biggest sellers because they're made better . . . packaged better! Acetate lenses are free from distortion. Ear pieces have hinge assemblies that will not break or fall off. High impact, virgin plastic frames with contrasting color decorations. The only giant glasses written up in double spread article in LIFE magazine. Packing and prices for every requirement. Order now!

A

LIFE Everybody's wearing 'em!
HOLLYWOOD
Spectaculars"
GIANT GLASSES

LIFE Everybody's wearing 'em!
HOLLYWOOD
Spectaculars"
GIANT GLASSES

B

A No. 690 "SUPER-SPECS"
New amazingly rich GOLD METALIZED FRAMES. TINTED sunglass lenses. Each in gift box. $2.00 retail.

No. 691 "SUPER-SPECS"
Same as above only with clear BIFOCAL lenses. $2.00 retail.

B No. 692 "SPECTACULARS"
High impact, virgin plastic frames with TINTED sunglass lenses. Boxed. $1.00 retail.

No. 693 "SPECTACULARS"
Same as above only with clear BIFOCAL lenses. $1.00 retail.

C 692/B "SPECTACULARS"
Same TINTED specs, but each in pliofilm bag with color header. $1.00 retail.

No. 693/B "SPECTACULARS"
Same as above only with clear BIFOCAL lenses. $1.00 retail.

C

H. FISHLOVE & CO.
712 NORTH FRANKLIN STREET, CHICAGO 10, ILLINOIS

©1960 H. F. & Co. Made in Chicago U.S.A.
PATENTS PENDING IN U.S.A. & FOREIGN COUNTRIES

with the overseas competitors' ersatz devices. Sales slackened further still as a result of the nosedive in global buzzer reputation and Joseph (Bud) Adams was forced to retool several years later, creating a superior product but essentially re-inventing the wheel at a price with which his company could survive.[xxv]

So exactly where did all those Joy Buzzers go when they left New Jersey or Hong Kong? The distribution channels of the industry were always somewhat catchall. These compact impulse purchases were sold nearly anywhere that foot traffic could be gathered. Manufacturers' salesmen hit the road year-round, aggressively developing new venues and hard-selling their latest sensations to the old ones. Product changed hands with consumer in dime stores, toy departments, magic shows, bus terminals, pitchmen's keisters, carnivals, circuses, roadside attractions, and the booming urban

downtown specialty outlets. By the mid-1940s, these dedicated joke and magic shops numbered approximately four thousand in the U.S. and reportedly grossed an annual business of $3,000,000 on items generally retailing for a quarter or less. Later, supermarkets, gift emporiums, and drugstores joined the feeding frenzy once canny manufacturers offered the previously unruly wares in ready—to—set-up spin-rack displays filled with bright, uniform, and tougher-to-shoplift blister packs. And currently, the World Wide Web is one-stop shopping for anyone on earth's Exploding Golf Ball or Revenge Toilet Paper needs.

Indeed, mail order itself always constituted a significant venue, and eventually came to be synonymous with this entire class of merchandise via the delirious Johnson Smith & Co. catalog (once described as "the Rosetta Stone of American culture" by humorist Jean Shepherd),[xxvi] easily the most exhaustive and enduring source. Salesman par excellence Alfred Johnson Smith began peddling rubber stamps and assorted novelties in Australia in 1905. He published his first catalog there in 1906, yet yearned to compete with the American midwestern catalog-giants Sears, Roebuck & Co. and Montgomery Ward & Co. By 1913, he was in Chicago and had founded the mail-order business that still bears his name (the name Johnson Smith & Co. sounded more like his

presumed rivals),[xxvii] already veering toward the unsavory items that the big boys eschewed.

Likened to the Sears, Roebuck catalog gone bad, the Johnson Smith volumes were more fat and more fun and more crammed with awful, wonderful, eye-poppingly illicit objects of desire than any one source imaginable until the advent of the Internet.

Heavily advertised in tabloids, Sunday supplements, pulps, hobby magazines, and comic books, these infinite compendiums of "things you never knew existed™" became a true fixture on the American scene, and Johnson Smith a household name to conjure with. And while Royal, Acme, Slack, King, Apex, Gem, Spors, United, Eagle, Magnotrix, Wilson, Gellman's, Western, Ellisdon's, State, M-G, Collins, Church, Anglin, Leachman's, R. W. Kellogg, Vic Lawston, Honor House, and untold thousands of other, similar mail-order empires rose from and bit the dust, Johnson Smith & Co. ("The Only Concern Of Its Kind In America") endured. The name and catalog became so inextricably linked to its products that much of its public imagined that the diabolical Mr. Johnson Smith himself brainstormed, designed, and manufactured every last celluloid flea in his annual encyclopedia of everything, while dictating the trademark avuncular, hyperbolic copy.

In fact, he very nearly did: Alfred

ENORMOUS VIBRATING EYE

You can almost hide yourself behind one of these enormous Vibrating Eyes. The inside of the eye is attached to a spring, which causes the eye to vibrate with every movement of the face. For a burlesque lecture or an eccentric characterisation these enormous Vibrating Eyes will be a most effective finishing touch.

No. 4356. Enormous Vibrating Eye **15c**
3 for 40c, or $1.35 per doz.

The Swollen Thumb

A most effective deception. It looks so painful it makes one shudder. It slips over your own thumb and will cause you to receive much sympathy from your friends. It can also be used as a finishing touch to a stage make up or disguise in amateur theatricals, etc.

No. 2108. Swollen Thumb. Price.....25c

BUNGED-UP EYE

Here's your chance, boys! Put on one of these bunged-up Eye Disguises. The effect as you enter the room is most bewildering. It is easily attached or detached in but a moment. Lots of fun.

No. 4355. Bunged-up Eye.........25c
3 for 65c, or $2.25 per doz.

Goozelem Goggles

If you want to be particularly fascinating you should have a pair of these Goozelem Goggles. Just an aristocratic style of pince-nez, but with a pair of handsome eyes set in the frames instead of glasses. By a slight movement of the head the eyeballs roll backward and forward in a most laughable manner. When wearing them you'd look so nice your best girl wouldn't recognize you. Try them.

No. 4379. Goozelem Goggles. Price **20c**

JOKE TEETH AND TONGUES

No. 4351. 10c.
Long Tongue

No. 4352. 15c.
Plate with 1 Tooth

No. 4353. 15c.
Joke Teeth with Tongue

These Joke Teeth and Tongues are just the thing to surprise your friends with. The tongues are extra long and quite ferocious looking, and produce the most comical effects. The celluloid plate fits in the mouth between the upper teeth and inside of upper lip that stays in position and does not interfere with speaking. No. 4351 is a long Tongue only. No. 4353 is long tongue and set of celluloid false teeth. No. 4352 is a joke plate with only one tooth showing. They are fine for amateur theatricals, etc.

No. 4351. Long Tongue. Price......10c
No. 4352. Plate with 1 Tooth.......15c
No. 4353. Joke Teeth with Tongue 15c

Trombone NOSE BLOWER
SOUNDS LIKE A FOG HORN

When some men blow their noses it sounds like a trombone. We have all got accustomed to those queer noises, but now the Nose Blower has come to torment us. It is ingeniously concealed in a handkerchief. On meeting your friends, or at a party, after chatting awhile, you carelessly take out your handkerchief and proceed to blow your nose. It's like a sudden clap of thunder. Hear the ladies scream, and some male friends will think they hear the whistle of a steam engine. Watch them put their fingers in their ears when they hear you blow your nose. **10c**
No. 2192. NOSE BLOWER. Price Postpaid
3 for 25c, or 75c per dozen Postpaid

Johnson Smith, the Bard of Chicago, Racine, and Detroit, himself wrote the bulk of the prose for these lovingly selected objects during the catalog's wildest, densest years, surely some of the most influential anonymous literature ever published. Johnson Smith & Co.'s singular voice and vision represents the authentic canon of a truly neglected American picture poet.[xxviii]

Visually retrofitted to accommodate a crazy quilt of manufacturers' stock cuts, recycled wood engravings, and in-house illustration of varying homogeny, the catalog itself stood out like an enormous, swollen, rubber thumb. It offered its captive audience a tantalizing peep into a strange, mysterious, and seemingly timeless world of primal retribution, shadowy mysticism, and unimaginably wicked fun, bewilderingly offset with the utmost in drab and mundane banalities. Only in the Borgesian world of Johnson Smith could you find the following items on sale in one location: celluloid babies in walnut shells; movie projectors; rubber mouse erasers; diamond rings; jockey costumes; hatbands that read "Let Me Tickle You"; .38 caliber revolvers; wisteria seeds; celluloid ears; live monogrammed turtles; silverware sets; compendiums of black magic; aluminum paint; Indian blankets; Jesus prints; brass knuckles; Dippy Birds; sneezing roses; egg timers; plastic warts; bejeweled glass bulldogs; rebuilt typewriters; shaving brushes; imitation vomit; and ukuleles. All happily coexisting on the pages, all equally valid consumer options, all equally mailable from Racine, Wisconsin, C.O.D. with no need for further explanation. The catalog continues some ninety years later—slim, colorful, only modestly diverting, yet still offering the palest whiff of the eternal.

We know comparatively little of the men and women who conceived, designed, and promoted these disreputable objects. One history that has survived is that of journeyman cartoonist Louis M. Glackens (1866–1933) and novelty emperor Soren Sorensen Adams (1869–1963)—an anonymous partnership that was integral to the look and the success of Alfred Johnson Smith's mail-order enterprise.

These two unsung friends were jointly responsible for both the steak and the sizzle of some of the most famous amusements in the world. Glackens was a well-known cartoonist and illustrator of his day, with work appearing regularly in *Puck*, the world's premier humor magazine. Significantly, he was also a seminal yet long-neglected pioneer of the comic strip (drawing the continuing weekly picture story "Hans and His Chums," among others, in the early 1900s) and the animated cartoon (creating his own short series of films during the 1910s for release by Bray Productions, W. R. Hearst's International Film Service, and other early production studios). By the mid-1910s, Glackens began supplying his newly prosperous buddy Sam with a series of hundreds of small cartoon panels,

(opposite) A typical Johnson Smith & Co. catalog page, 1930s.

(above) Ür text by the Bard of Chicago, Racine, and Detroit.

and the occasional elaborate catalog cover and illustration as well, beginning a collaboration that continued for decades. Joseph (Bud) Adams vividly recalled Mr. Glackens, the jovial, bad-toupee–wearing picture maker, taking his yearly working seaside vacation with the Adams clan, effortlessly delineating the latest flight of his papa's fiendish imagination before an ocean dip. These funny, raw-boned, economical, and joyously expressive spots usually depict the glorified Adams product in mid-bamboozle, beset upon a world of portly, balding, large-nosed gents in dinner jackets by lean, cagey, grinning wise-guys. The images were used in Adams's packaging, advertising, point-of-purchase displays, and catalogs, thus creating a look for the Adams product and, by extension, an entire industry that often helped itself to the use of Glackens's artwork along with Adams's gags. In another ironic practical joke of our schizoid culture's High/Low Art dichotomy, L. M. Glackens was the brother of none other than American master William Glackens (1870–1938), celebrated Ashcan School painter and member of "The Eight"—and the chairman for the selection of American art for the 1913 Armory show, where some of Louis's paintings hung as

well. While today William's canvases sell for minor fortunes and hang in every major collection of American art, Louis's work is still entertaining the millions on S. S. Adams packaging, and hangs in virtually every Main Street toy store and shopping mall in North America, where it changes hands for $4 or less. Most of us came to first know and first *want* these elusive objects only through the seemingly ancient, uncredited drawings of Glackens, which, long outlasting their original tasks, peppered the Johnson Smith gumbo for generations to come.

While the old jokes still paid off, the name of the game was "novelty," and the game meant turn-on-a-dime flexibility and a quick finger on the pulse of a fickle public, despite, by mid-century, an aging first generation of prankmen. In 1965, the seventy-something Sam Oumano proclaimed: "Oumano keeps up with the times. You can't stand still. More than fifty years I been in this business and I haven't stood still since."[xxix] And yet neither had the rules. Exploding cigars were first legislated against in 1916, when a fun-loving Pennsylvania coal miner beheaded his own personal "moocher." The FDA banned the original Cachoo formula in 1940. Adams adapted his

patented Bingo Shooting Device to the ridiculously appropriate application of land-mine detonation for the U.S. Army Ordinance Department during World War II,[xxx] perhaps enjoying some imagined personal revenge on Bingo's "Jap and German" patent moochers of previous decades. Self-protective joke-meisters would soon be soft-pedaling the shooting, fizzing, banging, and exploding ends of their businesses. By 1960, The Anarchist (Stink) Bomb was out, and Hollywood Super Specs were in. Edward M. Swartz, "the Ralph Nader of toy safety," published his damning *Toys That Don't Care* in 1971, followed by, naturally enough, *Toys That Kill*. By the mid-1970s, the Johnson Smith catalog, now run and written by second son Paul, had "dropped Itching Powder and almost everything applied to the skin or taken internally" and voluntarily subscribed to the Comics Code imprimatur, the American comic book industry's ignominious auto-vasectomy, quickly fashioned to save its own skin via a rigid code of censorship after the threatening Kefauver Congressional Committee investigation of 1954.[xxxi]

Product-liability insurance and nuisance lawsuits had long become part of the drill. Sam Adams died in 1962 at age eighty-four,

after years of semi-retirement, the most successful entrepreneur in the joy industry, but, not surprisingly, a somewhat less than joyous human being.[xxxii] While his conscientious successor, Joseph (Bud) Adams, continued to introduce new product and innovative merchandising, his major objective at the helm of S. S. Adams was to modernize production of the novelty company's increasingly important staples. "I've worked on the Joy Buzzer all my life to improve it. I made it better,"[xxxiii] confided the heroic Adams, who died at age eighty-three, in 2001. Today, Chris Adams, son of Bud, grandson of Sam, presides over the family legacy and the cavernous Neptune, New Jersey, factory where a core staff of twenty-six trained specialists continues daily to depress spring snakes into metal mixed-nut cans and test-drive Joy Buzzers until Miller time. "It's a stable business," reports Chris. "People always have money for a quick laugh."[xxxiv]

In the last few decades or so, bad taste has officially become both big business and High Art, and pranking a viable career option. The lowly, old-fashioned cheap laff has had to adapt or perish, in a world where the boundary lines of bad taste and pop-cultural chutzpah are routinely eroded on a sea-

(above) Undated (c. 1910–30s) catalog drawings for S. S. Adams by Louis M. Glackens.
(© 2004, S. S. Adams Company)

sonal basis. Hence, the three significant trends much of the industry has adopted: the Sexually Explicit (Franco-American offers a "spicy" line which includes a mustard jar with a shooting penis and a clockwork Happy Jerk-Off Clown); the High Tech (log onto www.johnsonsmith.com for a JPEG of the remote-control Whoopee Cushion); and the Geriatric (Over-the-Hill novelties for the aging baby boomer who never grew up). Significantly, another industry wrinkle has emerged as well, which must be labeled the Post-Modern. The Archie McPhee ("Since 1980") company of Seattle, self-proclaimed "Outfitters of Popular Culture," has successfully carried on the Johnson Smith torch with a low-key, self-reflexive, post-Warhol twist, aiming at an urban hipster contingent. It has also upped the ante on the viability of the Intentionally Ironic Manufactured Product (The Punching Nun Puppet, Sigmund Freud Action Figure, and a line of cute Parasite Pals girls' accessories), a mar-

keting gambit which dates back at least to the early-1960s ventures of the Milbit Manufacturing Co., with its Mink Eyebrows, not to mention Stupid Inc.'s Instant Panic aerosol, and which reached a perfection of sorts with the 1975 Pet Rock created by ad man Gary Dahl. The Shine Gallery of Los Angeles offers a slick, full-color, Art Deco-flavored catalog at five dollars a pop, framing vintage warehouse finds going back half a century at antique-mall prices. In an ultimate irony, Johnson Smith & Co. itself has spun off a niche-market catalog business mysteriously titled Betty's Attic, which specializes in deliberately kitschy, faux-retro nostalgia accoutrements. And Chris Adams, whose company's product line, as well as its merchandising and packaging, have not changed significantly in at least four decades, has effortlessly gained full market advantage of this latest development by standing squarely in place. Like the Johnson Smith Comic Clock (item #9721), the rules of the novelty game may have actually started running backward.

Yet before there were Jeff Koons and Howard Stern, Mel Brooks and John Waters, Garbage Pail Kids and Ren and Stimpy, there were millions of novelty creations filling a visceral and inexhaustible need. Vulgar, sadistic, stupid, odd, amusing, outlandish, brilliant, execrable, infantile, morbid, and exquisite, these artifacts represent the long-forgotten stock in the sub-basement of our culture. And, like the myriad layers of the human psyche, the deeper one digs, the more revealing it becomes.

S. S. Adams indulging in a cheap laff—
Newark Sunday Call, *March 22, 1942*

SURPRISE BOX—Ideal for puncturing windy after-dinner speakers. From a little box several dozen balls pop out.

i These products were in fact created and manufactured by competitor H. Fishlove & Co. ii Dale Shaw, "Big Boom in Old Boffs," *True Magazine*, October 1965 iii Joseph (Bud) Adams (S. S. Adams Co.), interview with John Kelly and Mark Newgarden, *XYY Magazine*, 1993 iv Helmut Schwarz, "History of the Nuremberg Toy Trade and Industry," *Journal of Social History*, 2003 v Richard O'Brian, *The Story of American Toys*, Abbeville Press, 1990 vi Maurice Zolotow, *It Takes All Kinds*, Random House, 1952 vii Rose Shamus, interview by Dan Nadel, 2004 viii Shaw, ibid ix ibid x Sol Pritt (Franco-American Novelty Co.), interview with Dan Nadel and Mark Newgarden, 2004 xi ibid xii Joel Sayre, "From Gags to Riches," *Scribners*, March 1941 xiii ibid xiv Pritt, ibid xv Sayre, ibid xvi Stan and Mardi Timm, "King of the Gag Boxes," *Games Magazine*, February 2003 xvii ibid xviii Chris Adams (S. S. Adams Co.), interview with Dan Nadel and Mark Newgarden, 2004 xix Maurice Zolotow, "The Jumping Snakes of S. S. Adams," *Saturday Evening Post*, June 1946 xx Sayre, ibid xxi Zolotow, *It Takes All Kinds*, ibid xxii Pritt, ibid xxiii Chris Adams, ibid xxiv Shaw, ibid xxv Robert A. Mamis, "Gross National Products," *Inc. Magazine*, April 1987 xxvi Jean Shepherd, *The 1929 Johnson Smith & Co. Catalogue*, Chelsea House, 1970 xxvii Betty Carrol, "Company Changes with the Times, Stays True to the Wacky, Weird," *Associated Press*, April 14, 2003 xxviii Stanley Elkin, "À la Recherche du Whoopee Cushion," *Pieces of Soap: Essays by Stanley Elkin*, Simon and Shuster, 1992 xxix Shaw, ibid xxx E. J. Tangerman, "Adam's Ribs Aren't Missing," *American Machinist*, August 15, 1946 xxxi Elkin, ibid xxxii William V. Rauscher, *S. S. Adams: High Priest of Pranks and Merchant of Magic*, 1878 Press Company, 2002 xxxiii Joseph (Bud) Adams, ibid xxxiv Chris Adams, ibid

S.S. ADAMS FACTORY TOUR
2004

In February, 2004, the authors made a pilgrimage to the S. S. Adams Company factory in Neptune, New Jersey. Virtually unchanged for over seventy years, the gags still roll off the manufacturing line in this cavernous space. Dormant signage and active gags were in abundance, as were (opposite, top left) Joy Buzzers in all stages of assemblage. Indeed, the buzzing of dozens of little Joy machines was ever present in this curious incubator of past and present laffs.

THE
LAFFS

IMITATION VOMIT

Amazingly realistic PUKE! Looks like someone was SICK, SICK, SICK! almost turns your stomach to use as joke, it's so realistic. Made of plastic. The "gloppiest" look. Place by baby, dog, dinner table or pretend you've been sick. Most revolting, dirtiest trick we've seen.

☐ 2636. Price Postpaid .... **50¢**

IMITATION VOMIT

AKA *Whoops, Glop, Oops, Fake Vomit*

DIMENSIONS 4" x 5" (depending on orientation)

ORIGINATOR Marvin Glass & Associates, for H. Fishlove & Co., c. 1950s (Whoops)

DATE OF MANUFACTURE c. 1960s

DESCRIPTION Realistic (apparently modeled on an orange-juice and chili diet) spurious discharge

MAKER Anonymous (Unpackaged example purchased from Johnson Smith & Co., 1969)

SLOGAN "Amazingly realistic PUKE!" (Johnson Smith & Co. catalog)

INSTRUCTIONS Behold (implicit)

UTILITY Best left on temporary display in well-traveled area

TARGET AUDIENCE The author, age 9

ORIGINAL RETAIL PRICE 50¢

NOTES "Fishlove was the premier joke and gag manufacturer of the times and they were a client of Marvin Glass [creators of Yakity-Yak Talking Teeth and Super Specs]. Marvin was preparing a presentation of new items. A designer (I wish I remembered his name) came up with the totally original idea of fake vomit. He showed it to Marvin and Marvin hated it. 'That's disgusting, you're sick, there is nothing funny about it,' shouted Marvin Glass. The presentation with Fishlove was not going anywhere. Several items were met with polite interest but nothing more. The fake-vomit designer then burst through the conference room door and slapped the PUKE squarely on the table in front of the client. You can imagine Marvin's face. Fishlove was laughing hysterically and clearly loved it. Marvin immediately piped up, 'Yes, this is great! That's why we saved it for last. We love it!' and Marvin sold it to the client like it was the greatest thing ever."—Erick Erickson, toy designer, 2004

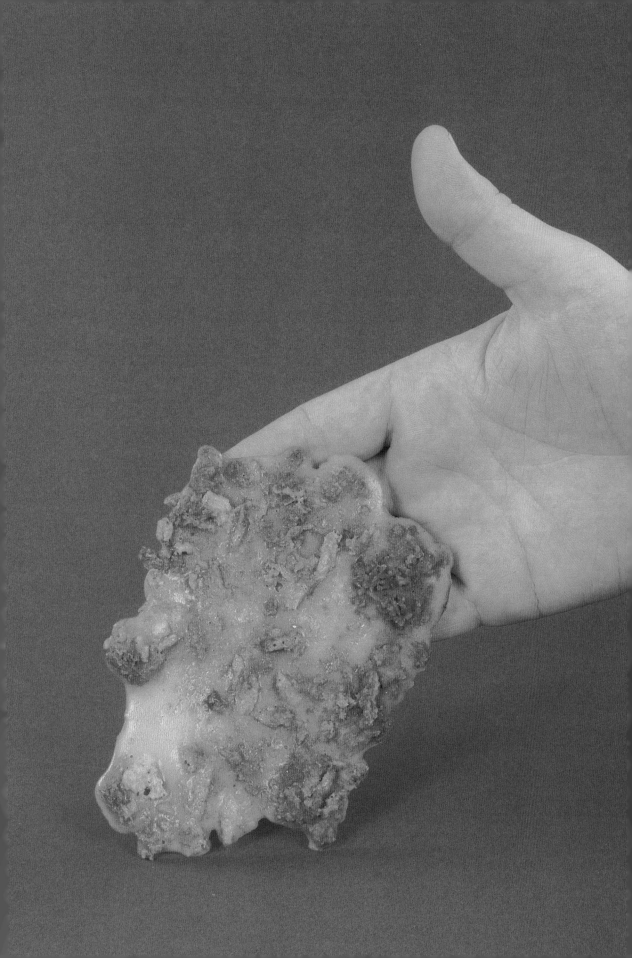

MYSTERY GRAB BAG

AKA	*Surprise Package, Box O Jokes, Barrel O Fun, Surprise Parcel, Big Joke Box, Grab Bag Assortment*
DIMENSIONS	6³⁄₄" x 3¹⁄₈"
PACKAGE	Red cloth bag, printed in one color, with stitched drawstring
ORIGINATOR	Unknown
DATE OF MANUFACTURE	c. 1940s
DESCRIPTION	Parcel allegedly containing eighteen articles (Novelties? Tricks? Toys? Trinkets? Puzzles? Games? Prizes?)
MAKER	Anonymous retailer (Made in U.S.A.)
SLOGAN	"18 Articles in This Bag!"
INSTRUCTIONS	None
UTILITY	Provides unwary consumer vague hope for novelty bargains
TARGET AUDIENCE	Mail-order gamblers
ORIGINAL RETAIL PRICE	Unknown
NOTES	Despite the high ideals of this enterprise and a legitimate desire to educate a novelty-info–craving public, after much debate, soul searching, and inner struggle, the author has decided that the actual contents of the Mystery Grab Bag should best remain a public mystery, as envisioned by its sage creators.

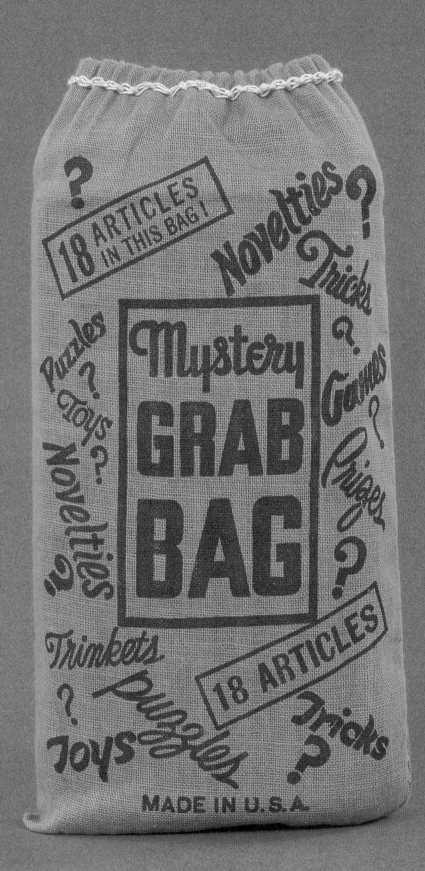

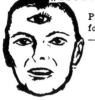

#25500 THIRD EYE

Press it on to the forehead it will stick —its realistic too.

TRICK EYE SUCTION CUP

AKA   *The Third Eye, Extra Eye*

DISPLAY DIMENSIONS   3" x 2 1/2"

EYE DIMENSIONS   1 3/4" x 1 1/4"

PACKAGE   Polyethylene bag, double–saddle-stitched onto cardboard header, printed in three colors

ORIGINATOR   Unknown

DATE OF MANUFACTURE   c. 1970s

DESCRIPTION   Molded-plastic orbicularis oculi and orb with spot-glued, 1/2"-around, two-stage lenticular iris and 3/4"-around rubber suction cup on reverse

MAKER   Unknown (Made in Hong Kong)

SLOGAN   None

INSTRUCTIONS   "DIRECTIONS: Place on forehead/for a real laugh/can also be set on/a whiskey glass"

UTILITY   Removable prosthetic approximation of an animated eye

TARGET AUDIENCE   Bald gentlemen with excessively high foreheads (implicit)

ORIGINAL RETAIL PRICE   Unknown

NOTES   In Eastern Yoga practices, the physiological site of the sixth and highest chakra (or sahasrara) is located in the center of the forehead and is symbolized by the so-called "third eye." When this eye is opened, a new and completely other dimension of reality is revealed to the practitioner. The psychic trauma implicit in a constantly flickering third eye could be of considerable negative consequence to a novice. Perhaps this is why the cautious manufacturer provided directions that gently nudge the user toward the comparatively harmless application on a glass of whiskey.

THE FUNNY DRIBBLE GLASS

AKA	*The Famous Dribble Glass, The Trick Glass, The Dribble Juice Glass, The Dribble Wine Glass, The Dribble Water Glass, Gordon's Dribble Glass, Enardoe's Funny Dribble Glass, Dribbler's Glass*
DISPLAY DIMENSIONS	4 1/8" x 3"
GLASS DIMENSIONS	3 3/4" x 2 1/2"
PACKAGE	Heavy-gauge tube cardboard covered in paper, printed in one color
ORIGINATOR	Samuel Sorenson Adams, 1909
DATE OF MANUFACTURE	c. 1920s
DESCRIPTION	Drinking glass with small holes concealed in sand-blasted grape-leaf pattern
MAKER	S. S. Adams Co., Neptune, New Jersey
SLOGAN	"A Harmless Though Very Funny Joke"
INSTRUCTIONS	"This is a trick glass; the leaves are cut all the way through the sides of the glass. The contents will flow through these holes and will trickle down the chin and shirtfront of anyone who drinks from it. The victims usually think that the fault is their own; they will wipe off their cheeks and invariably will try again and again."
UTILITY	Vessel of trustworthy appearance that surreptitiously sprinkles liquid refreshment on "victim"
TARGET AUDIENCE	Whimsical hosts of thirsty friends
ORIGINAL RETAIL PRICE	25¢
NOTES	The original "table prank" and the great stealth bomber in any serious practical joker's arsenal. A staple product for the tumbler's originator, with varying models in continuous manufacture since 1909.

21 INSULT CARDS. Latest rage at parties, gatherings, in offices, on the street, etc. Very hilarious! The funniest insults you ever read! Even the grouchiest folks perk up and roar with laughter at these. Will tickle your funny-bone too. Take out some life insurance in case you laugh yourself to death over these. Keep handy in pocket for fun anytime — anyplace.
Cat. No. 1764. Price... **35¢**

COMIC CARDS

AKA	*Insult Cards, Fun Cards, Gag Cards, Hecklers' Cards, Motto Cards, Acquaintance Cards, Comical Calling Cards, Crazy Calling Cards, Wallet Sized America's Newest Comic Cards, Hot Air Wise Crack Cards, Red Hot Shots, Craphouse Wisecracks, Lovers Fun Card Set, Novelty Visiting Cards, Sheik Cards, Stag Fun Package Cards, Get Aquainted Name and Game Cards, Luminous Fun Cards*
CARD DIMENSIONS	2" x 3½"
ORIGINATOR	Unknown
DATE OF MANUFACTURE	c. 1940s–1950s
DESCRIPTION	Paper cards, printed with humorous message in one color
MAKER	NOOT, The Printer, Compton, California, et al.
SLOGAN	None
INSTRUCTIONS	Present directly to targeted audience (implicit)
UTILITY	Achieves insult instantly without necessity for spontaneity, wit, or verbal effort
TARGET AUDIENCE	Enemies of insult-worthy individuals who can read
ORIGINAL RETAIL PRICE	Unknown
NOTES	Anonymously authored and cheaply printed, "insult" or "comic" cards like these proliferated throughout the twentieth century, perhaps an unknown gag-mechanic's marriage between the gentleman's calling card and the Victorian "vinegar [insult] valentine." Descendants of these primal endeavors include the "funny" greeting card, the churlish barroom plaque, the "wise-guy" bubblegum card, and the photocopied office-humor sheet, all of which imbibe from the same inbred gene pool of low-brow aphorisms.

Do It Tomorrow

you've made enough mistakes today

Is Already Made Up

Don't
Confuse
Me
With
The
Facts

I'd Like To Help You Out

which way did you come in

IF YOU DON'T STOP ANNOYING ME, I'M GOING TO TAKE THE GAS PIPE, AND PUT IT RIGHT IN YOUR MOUTH

IT'S NOT THAT I'M HARD OF HEARING

IT'S JUST THAT I DON'T WANT TO

LISTEN TO YOU

Our Eyes Have Met
Our Lips Not Yet
But You Can Bet
I'll Get Them Yet

I Am not A very fast truckdriver

I Am not A very slow truckdriver

I Am just A haffast truckdriver.

The Service was EXCELLENT

This TIP to thank you

MONEY ISN'T EVERYTHING

BUT IT'S AWAY AHEAD OF WHATEVER IS IN SECOND PLACE

I'm Never Too Busy

TO SAY "NO"

COMPLIMENTS OF: NOOT, THE PRINTER
44 BULLIS ROAD (THE STREET BEHIND SEARS) COMPTON
12 TO 6 DAILY   NE. 2-5679   SAT. 10 TO 4

Chance
This Card May Be Kept Until Needed Or Sold

GET OUT OF JAIL FREE

Courtesy Of:

• Rose BIRD • Joseph GRODIN
• Cruz REYNOSO • Stanley MOSK

---

my card

IF IT'S HONEST . . .

I DON'T WANT TO HAVE ANYTHING TO DO WITH IT

I'd Like To Compliment You On Your Work

. . when will you start?

Your Story Has Touched
My Heart
Never Before Have I Met Anyone
With More Troubles Than You Have.
Please Accept This Token
Of My Sincere Sympathy.

We Welcome Criticism

write your's here

HOW?

Mistakes Will Happen

But Must You Give Them
So Much Help?

Consider This Day
Total Loss ------

Unless I Receive HELL
From Someone

If I had an eraser,
I'd rub you out!

THE GEOGRAPHICAL AGES OF WOMEN

FROM 15 TO 25: She is Like Africa.
Half Virgin, Half Explored.

FROM 25 TO 35: She is like Asia.
Hot, Torrid, and Mysterious.

FROM 35 TO 45: She is like America.
Streamlined, Efficient, Cooperative.

FROM 45 TO 55: She is like Europe.
Devastated, but still Good.

AFTER 55, She is like Australia
Everyone knows where it is, but nobo goes there.

I don't neck with everybody -

Love Your Enemy

YOU MAY THINK YOU'RE THE BIG CHEESE
AROUND HERE—BUT

TRICK SMOKING MONKEY W/CIGARETTES

AKA	*The Smoking Monkey, Smoking Pets, Smokie Pets, Mysterious Smoking Pets, Loveable Smoking Traveler's Pet, Puffing Billy, Smokie The Mule, Smokie Skull, Smoking Skeleton*
VENDING DISPLAY DIMENSIONS	12 1/2" x 7 7/8"
PACKAGE DIMENSIONS	3 3/4" x 2 5/8"
MONKEY DIMENSIONS	1 3/4" x 1"
PACKAGE	Polyethylene bag, double-saddle-stitched onto cardboard, printed in four colors
DESCRIPTION	Blow-molded hollow-plastic monkey with 1/16"-diameter mouth hole, packaged together with 7–8 paper "ciga-rettes" in plastic bag and header card combination
ORIGINATOR	Unknown (U.S. Patent No. 465,031)
DATE OF MANUFACTURE	c. 1960s
MAKER	Anonymous (Made in Japan)
SLOGAN	None
INSTRUCTIONS	"Place Cigarette in Monkeys [sic] Mouth/Light it and Watch Him Smoke"
UTILITY	Creates apparently noteworthy experience of witnessing plastic monkey smoking
TARGET AUDIENCE	Those young enough to want plastic monkeys yet old enough to want to light matches
ORIGINAL RETAIL PRICE	Unknown
NOTES	Performing simians trained to smoke have captivated mankind since antiquity. The mysteriously compelling motif has been revisited over the centuries in paintings, prints, French automata, and German clockwork toys. These latter-day descendants, complete with "magic cig-arettes," date to the early 1960s. Their appearance on the dime store scene was preceded by a flap of similar plastic smoking pets that in turn emerged from the imported ceramic novelty animal ashtrays and incense figurines popular in the preceding decades.

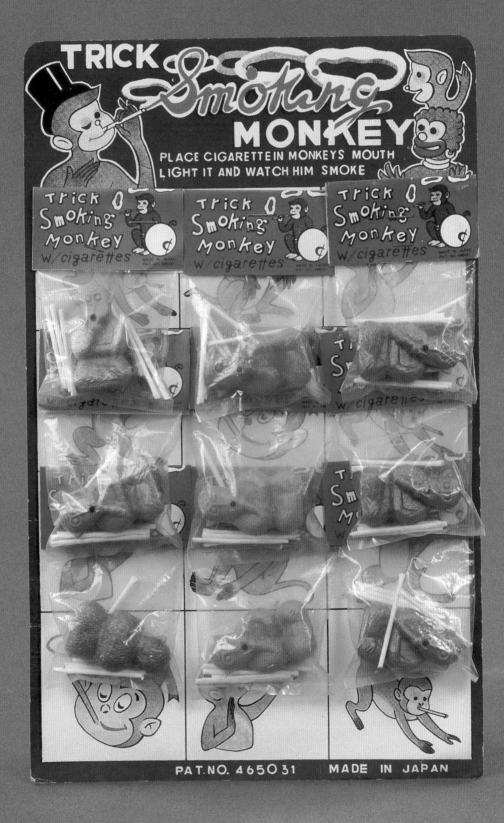

SWISS CHEESE

This piece of Swiss Cheese is made of
plastic material and is so flexible and so
realistic-looking that the recipient will
definitely mistake this imitation for the
real cheese. Can you imagine what hap-
pens when this piece of cheese is put between two piece of bread and the victim
takes a bite.

Dozen $1.50 — Gross $17.50

PLASTIC SWISS CHEESE

AKA   *Phony Cheese*

WRAPPER DIMENSIONS	4¼" x 4¼"
CHEESE DIMENSIONS	4¼" x 4¼"
PACKAGE	Tissue paper, triple-wrapped, printed in two colors
ORIGINATOR	Unknown
DATE OF MANUFACTURE	c. 1950 (Japan)
DESCRIPTION	Limp, thin, polymer square in paper wrapper
MAKER	Anonymous (Made in Japan)
SLOGAN	"Place this imitation Swiss cheese between two slices of bread serve this and watch the fun."
INSTRUCTIONS	"Place this imitation Swiss cheese between two slices of bread serve this and watch the fun."
UTILITY	"Place this imitation Swiss cheese between two slices of bread serve this and watch the fun."
TARGET AUDIENCE	Fun-watching friends of the Swiss-cheese hungry
ORIGINAL RETAIL PRICE	Unknown
NOTES	"We got anything you could name to make you laugh. Fake ham, fake cheese, fake blood, fake hot dogs, and a fake ice cube with a real bug inside!"—Sam Oumano, Franco-American Novelty Co., 1965

Jumping Match Box Stand

There should be no lack of opportunity to work this joke off on your male acquaintances. It is a combination match box holder and ash tray, and as such will be found extremely useful. Upon attempting to light a match, a catch releases a spring and a cleverly hidden contrivance inside causes the matches to jump out of the box and fly in all directions. The article is well made entirely of metal, elegantly painted in red.

No. 2729. Jumping Match Box Stand. 75c

JUMPING MATCH STAND

AKA	*Jumping Match Box Stand*
DIMENSIONS	$3^1/8$" x $1^5/8$" x $3^1/4$" around (bowl)
ORIGINATOR	Unknown
DATE OF MANUFACTURE	c. 1920s
DESCRIPTION	Nickle-plated metal ashtray, connected to spring-loaded match dispenser with frontal tin plate, lithographed in two colors; mechanism triggered by striking match on side surface
MAKER	Anonymous (Made in Germany)
SLOGAN	Unknown
INSTRUCTIONS	Set spring-coiled false bottom in decoy matchbox, add stick matches, wait in prey for unsuspecting quarry (implicit)
UTILITY	Creates havoc and anxiety via normally inert table dressing
TARGET AUDIENCE	Crafty hosts visited by skittish match users
ORIGINAL RETAIL PRICE	Unknown
NOTES	A ruggedly made German hoot which had become a somewhat archaic import by the 1930s, with the proliferation of folding safety matchbooks in America replacing the European-favored stick matches.

H. FISHLOVE & COMPANY
712-720 North Franklin Street
Chicago 10, Illinois

now see this!

FORM 3547 REQUESTED

HOLLYWOOD SUPER–SPECS

AKA	*Hollywood Spectaculars, Giant Glasses, Mammoth Spectacles, Giant Specs, Jumbo Comic Specs*
BOX DIMENSIONS	11½" x 4⅛" x 1¾"
SPECS DIMENSIONS	11¼" x 3¾" x 7¼" (unfolded)
PACKAGE	Paper-covered cardboard box, printed in two colors, polypropylene inner wrap
ORIGINATOR	Marvin Glass & Associates for H. Fishlove & Co., Chicago (Pat. Pending)
DATE OF ORIGIN	1960
DESCRIPTION	Larger than necessary—by far—plastic eyewear, molded in marbelized plastic, with attached tinted-plastic lenses
MAKER	H. Fishlove & Co., Chicago (#690—tinted)
SLOGAN	"Comical! Astonishing! Largest, funniest glasses ever made!" "As seen in *Life Magazine*"
INSTRUCTIONS	Apply to bridge of nose and behind helix of outer ear in the manner of regularly proportioned, non-comical, non-astonishing eyeglass frames (implicit)
UTILITY	Wearer presumably creates comical juxtaposition resulting in astonishment of onlookers
TARGET AUDIENCE	Game individuals frequenting "sports, beach, conventions, office, school, motoring and parties" with minimal concern for foolish affect
ORIGINAL RETAIL PRICE	95¢
NOTES	Exemplary of the industry sub-genre known as The Comedic Oversized Personal Effect. Other perennials include: oversized erasers; hats; combs; toothbrushes; and mice. Brainchild of famed toy-design guru Marvin Glass & Associates, these and similar Fishlove spawn served as middle-world intermediaries between the pop-cultural poles of F. W. Woolworth and Claes Oldenburg.

BEATNIK BEARD

AKA	*Beatnik Goatee, Beatnik Disguise, Bob Russel's Beatnik Goatee*
DISPLAY DIMENSIONS	6½" x 4¾"
BEARD DIMENSIONS	4" x 2"
PACKAGE	Cardboard header, printed in one color, double–saddle-stitched to polyethylene bag
ORIGINATOR	Unknown
DATE OF MANUFACTURE	c. 1960s
DESCRIPTION	Rabbit-fur chin piece, machine-stitched onto plastic inner lining with applied adhesive
MAKER	Anonymous
SLOGAN	"Dig That Beard! Crazy Man!"
INSTRUCTIONS	"Self Adhering!"
UTILITY	Necessary in preparation for camouflaging oneself as a "beatnik"
TARGET AUDIENCE	Non-beatniks
ORIGINAL RETAIL PRICE	$1.29
NOTES	The word "beatnik" (from Jack Kerouac's "Beat Generation" and the U.S.S.R.'s "Sputnik") was apparently first coined on April 2, 1958, by San Francisco *Chronicle* columnist Herb Caen. The disparaging label, as applied to the younger generation's latest crop of self-styled outcasts, stuck hard and outlived that generation's rebellion several times over. The signature unkempt facial hair, essential to the hip outsider's uniform, was codified via the high-profile caricature of Bob Denver as Maynard G. Krebs on the CBS-TV prime-time hit "The Many Loves of Dobie Gillis" (1959–1963). "Beatnik" disguises are still readily available today and still marketed as such, despite the virtual extinction of any practicing specimens.

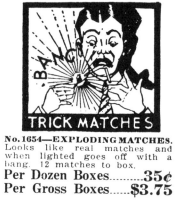

No. 1654—EXPLODING MATCHES.
Looks like real matches and
when lighted goes off with a
bang. 12 matches to box.

Per Dozen Boxes.........35¢
Per Gross Boxes......$3.75

JOKERS FOR SMOKERS – BANG MATCHES

AKA	*Exploding Matches, Trick Matches, Explosive Book Matches, Shooting Matches, Sparkling Matches, Bingo Matchbook, Bango Matchbook*
VENDING DISPLAY DIMENSIONS	10¼" x 5"
MATCHBOOK DIMENSIONS	1⅞" x ½" x ⅜"
PACKAGE	Folded cardboard matchbook printed in one color, saddle-stitched with applied "front striker" abrasive strip
ORIGINATOR	Unknown
DATE OF MANUFACTURE	c. 1950s
DESCRIPTION	Matchbook (decorated stock cut from the Match Corporation of America) containing both standard-issue and mercury-fulminate–enhanced-tip matches
MAKER	Anonymous
SLOGAN	"Fool the Moochers"
INSTRUCTIONS	"The back row is regular, the front row is BANG! YOU light up with a regular match from back. YOUR VICTIM takes one from the front row—BANG!"
UTILITY	Reserve arsenal for vengeance-minded smokers
TARGET AUDIENCE	Match carriers regularly beset by "the Moochers"
ORIGINAL RETAIL PRICE	10¢
NOTES	The number of burn wards filled via unexpected encounters with Jokers for Smokers is unrecorded and unrecordable. Joseph (Bud) Adams of the S. S. Adams Co. disclosed in a 1993 interview that he "bumped heads" with his father, Sam, over the manufacture of these potentially hazardous products and was personally responsible for the discontinuation of such risky offerings from that company's line in the early 1940s.

THE MAGIC NAIL.

A very good and low-priced trick. A common iron nail is shown and without a moment's hesitation the performer forces it through his finger. The finger is shown with the nail protruding from both sides. The illusion is so perfect that the spectators will be satisfied that the wound is a genuine one, and that the nail really goes through the finger. The next instant the nail is withdrawn, given for examination, and the finger shown, without a cut, scar or wound of any kind. Price, 15 cents, post-paid. One dozen, $1.00.

TRICK NAIL IN FINGER

AKA	*The Great Nail Trick, Nail Thru Finger, The Magic Nail, The Mystic Nail*
DIMENSIONS	2⅜" x ⅛"
ORIGINATOR	Unknown
DATE OF MANUFACTURE	c. 1960s
DESCRIPTION	Rusty nail with semi-circular bend, red paint applied
MAKER	Anonymous
SLOGAN	Unknown
INSTRUCTIONS	None
UTILITY	Worn finger-in-groove from behind, to achieve the illusion of nail piercing flesh
TARGET AUDIENCE	Children or other persons of a particular finger size
ORIGINAL RETAIL PRICE	Unknown
NOTES	A timeless illusion, the pictured object is the last remaining fragment of a treasured childhood magic set.

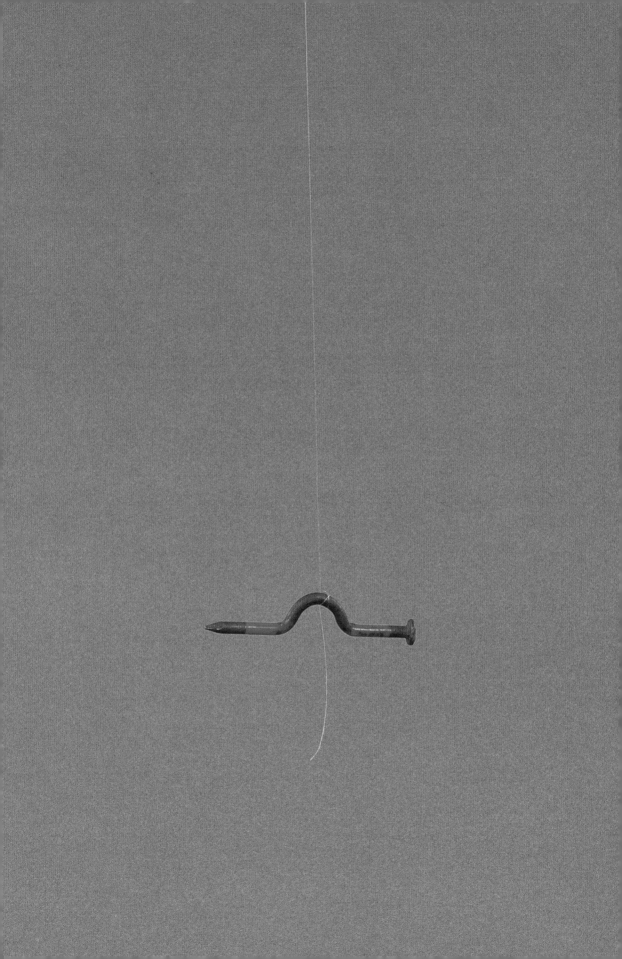

Moaner's CRYING TOWELS

Next time any one cries about business, love, politics, bad cards, bum golf, depressions, hard luck or religion; when he says the world's "all wet" and "life simply ain't worth living," just hand him one of these Crying Towels and watch him smile through those tears. There are six paper towels in an envelope, each with the following inscription: "STOP MOANING. Dry Up Your Tears. Laugh And The World Laughs With You. Weep And You Weep Alone."

No. 2852. Crying Towels, Pkg. 6 . . **15c**

CRYING TOWEL

AKA   *Moaner's Crying Towels*

DIMENSIONS   15½" x 25"
ORIGINATOR   Unknown
DATE OF MANUFACTURE   c. 1950s
DESCRIPTION   Linen, printed in four colors
MAKER   Unknown
SLOGAN   "It Absorbs All Troubles"

INSTRUCTIONS   Hold to face and weep into towel (implicit)
UTILITY   "It Absorbs All Troubles"
TARGET AUDIENCE   Presenters of consolation or booby prizes for deserving recipients
ORIGINAL RETAIL PRICE   Unknown

NOTES   The crying towel, presaged by the spurious fourth-century Christian relic known as Veronica's Veil, seems to have proliferated as one-stop gag-gift venue in the post-World War II years. Hundreds, if not thousands, of off-the-rack designs exist, commemorating and offering ineffectual succor to every category of "loser" on the American landscape: golfers; bowlers; fishermen; hunters; vacationers; baseball players; photographers; buck privates; dieters; investors; horseplayers; cardplayers; drinkers; drunks; kibitzers; mothers; fathers; mothers-in-law; fathers-in-law; newlyweds; and even Alaska state residents. However, to date, no crying towels have been discovered that are devoted to the sorry lot of shoestring novelty manufacturers or anonymous crying-towel illustrators.

	Price per Dozen	Jobbers Price per Gross

No. 618 Talking Teeth
Regulation size imitation false teeth made of plastic. Operated by a spring motor which makes the teeth open and close same as when person is talking, also chatter and move around. Packed individually in colorful box. A display card with each dozen.

$7.20 $64.80

YAKITY-YAK TALKING TEETH

AKA	*Talking Teeth, Amazing Talking False Teeth, Chatter-Chatter Teeth, Hopping Teeth, Funny Teeth, Over The Hill Talking Dentures*
BOX DIMENSIONS	$3\frac{3}{8}$" x $3\frac{3}{8}$" x $1\frac{3}{8}$"
TEETH DIMENSIONS	$2\frac{1}{2}$" x $2\frac{1}{2}$" x $1\frac{1}{2}$"
PACKAGE	Cardboard box, printed in two colors
ORIGINATOR	Adolph Goldfarb, Marvin Glass & Associates for H. Fishlove & Co. (U.S. Patent No. 2,504,679, November 24, 1948)
DATE OF MANUFACTURE	c. 1950s
DESCRIPTION	Hinged, key-wind, plastic dental plates
MAKER	H. Fishlove & Co., Chicago
SLOGAN	"Amazing! They Walk! They Talk! They're Alive!"
INSTRUCTIONS	"1. After winding conceal the teeth in your hand. Set them down on a smooth surface among a group of talkative people with an exclamation 'All you do is yakity-yak.' 2. Pretend to take the teeth out of your mouth then holding them by the bottom plate let them 'talk' by themselves."
UTILITY	Portable, independently animated dentrifice
TARGET AUDIENCE	1. Those demonstrably critical of talkative people 2. Fun-loving oral-decay victims prone to sleight of hand
ORIGINAL RETAIL PRICE	Unknown
NOTES	First manufactured in 1949 by the fabled Chicago outfit H. Fishlove & Co., and designed for Marvin Glass & Associates by Adolph (Eddy) Goldfarb, who credited his mother-in-law as the muse for his inspiration. Sol Pritt on H. Fishlove & Co.: "Irving was the founder, and Howard took over. He was not an Irving. Irving was funny. A great guy. Could be very humorous. He would travel all over the world and when he came back he would have a theme party at his house based on the country he just returned from. He loved being funny. He was a real funny man. He was made for this business." Yakity-Yak is still produced today to the same high specifications by Fun Inc. of Chicago, yet, sadly, only a few thousand sets of these classic choppers chatter out the Fun Inc. shipping doors per annum.

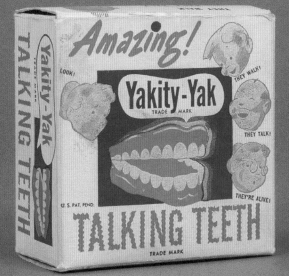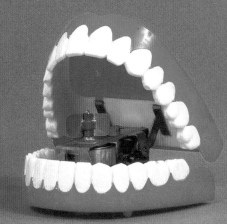

FANCY RUBBER NOSES
(Assorted)

With stickons rubber noses that will stay on the nose. P. S. Inside is a double sided tape to hold the rubber nose onto the nose.

NOSEY-NOVELTY

AKA — *Rubber Nose, Fancy Rubber Noses, Big Nose, Shnoz, Snoz, False Nose, Mr. Schnozz, Durante Nose*

DISPLAY CARD DIMENSIONS — 5 1/2" x 7"

NOSE DIMENSIONS — 2 1/2" x 2 1/4" x 1"

PACKAGE — Cardboard, printed in four colors

ORIGINATOR — Unknown

DATE OF MANUFACTURE — c. 1960

DESCRIPTION — Spray-tinted rubber nose with twin, double-sided adhesive patches applied, saddle-stitched to display card

MAKER — Unknown (Encircled "E" logo; Made in U.S.A.)

SLOGAN — "Fun For All! *101 Laughs*"

INSTRUCTIONS — "Just stick it on! Remove Backing on Adhesive"

UTILITY — Provides user with the "fun" of a larger-than-average (by 125–150%) proboscis

TARGET AUDIENCE — All

ORIGINAL RETAIL PRICE — 29¢

NOTES — Bastard offspring of the culturally higher-profile "big nose and glasses" combo, this attractive model was presumably an easier fit for the spectacle-wearing market segment in search of whimsical nasal adornment.

JUCK-PULVER/ITCHING-POWDER

AKA   *Itch Powder*

ENVELOPE DIMENSIONS   4³/₄" x 2¹/₄"

POWDER DIMENSIONS   Unknown

PACKAGE   Paper envelope, printed in two colors

ORIGINATOR   Samuel Sorenson Adams, c. 1904

DATE OF MANUFACTURE   c. 1970s

DESCRIPTION   Envelope of unspecified white powder

MAKER   Unknown ("Z" trademark; No. 9016, Made in Germany)

SLOGAN   "Another good practical joke" (catalog description, 1930s)

INSTRUCTIONS   Administer to general area of intended effect (implicit)

UTILITY   Creates skin irritation upon deployment

TARGET AUDIENCE   Stealthy humorist able to gain discreet access to dupe's unexposed derma

ORIGINAL RETAIL PRICE   Unknown

NOTES   "Itching powder has put people in the hospital. It's made from a weed grown in India. If any cattle get into that weed they have to be destroyed. They go crazy."—Joseph (Bud) Adams, 1993

MIMI THE SNAPPY BUBBLE DANCER

AKA	*Mademoiselle Fatima, Miss Lola, Miss Lolo, The Naked Truth, Snapper Joke, Snapping Gum Trick*
DIMENSIONS	3 7/8" x 2"
ORIGINATOR	Unknown
DATE OF MANUFACTURE	c. 1930s
DESCRIPTION	Cardboard sleeve, printed in two colors, with die-cut tab partially enclosing die-cut cardboard inner sleeve; attached low-tension metal-wire snapping mechanism on reverse
MAKER	Unknown (Japan)
SLOGAN	"For Men Only"
INSTRUCTIONS	Set wire trap, offer Mimi to sucker for closer inspection, run! (implicit)
UTILITY	Miniature, morally based behavior-modification device
TARGET AUDIENCE	Men only
ORIGINAL RETAIL PRICE	Unknown
NOTES	The subject of this 1930s Japanese-made variation on earlier French and German models refers to the provocative "Bubble Dance" striptease popularized by Sally Rand at the 1934 Chicago "Century of Progress" World's Fair. Later, less salacious models, aiming squarely at a kid consumer base, replaced the lure of a peep at naked limbs with a chaste stick of Wrigley's gum.

INK BOTTLE & BLOT
Put this on table-cloth or set of opened books and watch the victim scream blue murder! It certainly appears as if the bottle of ink has spilled. **Boxed, 25c**

INK BOTTLE AND INK SPOT

AKA	*Fake Ink Blot, Imitation Ink Bottle and Blot, Ink Bottle & Blot, Ink Blot Joke, Trick Ink Spill*
BOX DIMENSIONS	2¼" x 3¼" x 2⅝"
BOTTLE DIMENSIONS	2½" x 1½" x 1½"
SPILL DIMENSIONS:	1" x 3"
PACKAGE	Cardboard box, printed in one color
ORIGINATOR	Unknown (some sources credit Samuel Sorenson Adams)
DATE OF MANUFACTURE	c. 1940
DESCRIPTION	Glass ink bottle (empty, with painted interior) with applied paper label, printed in two colors, packaged with plastic black-ink "spill"
MAKER	"R. A. [Richard Appel Co., N.Y.] 429 (Made in U.S.A)"
SLOGAN	None
INSTRUCTIONS	"Place on a table top, books, or stationery—and watch the fun start"
UTILITY	Instant accident scene
TARGET AUDIENCE	Fun-instigators in home, school, and library
ORIGINAL RETAIL PRICE	Unknown
NOTES	The gleeful little fellow with the kidney-bean profile pictured on the top of this box was billed as "Jo King" and graced the packages, counter displays, and advertisements of scores of novelty items produced in the 1940s and '50s by the Richard Appel Co., once considered S. S. Adams's arch-rival. This long-time boff was recently updated for office hijinks as "Liquid Paper Spill."

INK BOTTLE
AND
INK SPOT

LAUGHING COMIC TISSUE
This is a small roll of regulation size toilet paper. On each sheet is printed very comical verses and witty sayings. Nothing obscene but very clever. 6 kinds such as "Snappy Snaps" "Bathroom Bullosophy'", "Polluted Proverbs", "Tummy Ticklers", "Ticker Bull", "Mother Goose Rhymes". **25c Roll**

LAFF TISSUE

AKA	*Laughing Tissue, Laugh Tissue Rolls, Laffin' Tissue, Laughing Toilet Paper Roll, Laughing Comic Tissue, Comic Toilet Tissue, The Morning Paper, Victory Morning Paper, After Dinner Roll*
BOX DIMENSIONS	5" x 4½" x 4½"
TISSUE DIMENSIONS	4½" around x 4¼"
PACKAGE	Cardboard gift box with paper display insert, printed in one color
ORIGINATOR	Samuel Sorenson Adams
DATE OF MANUFACTURE	1959
DESCRIPTION	Roll of tissue paper on cardboard tube, imprinted in succession, with over six thousand gag cartoons
MAKER	S. S. Adams Co., Asbury Park, New Jersey
SLOGANS	"Delightfully Delirious, Daringly Dizzy!" "Something Your Fun Loving Friends Really Will Enjoy!"
INSTRUCTIONS	Unroll, laff, wipe, repeat (implicit)
UTILITY	Recreational as well as functional cartoon literature
TARGET AUDIENCE	Friends of fun-loving, defecating friends
ORIGINAL RETAIL PRICE	Unknown
NOTES	According to William V. Rauscher in his 2002 biography *S. S. Adams: High Priest of Pranks and Merchant of Magic*, after Adams's death in 1963, the South Jersey novelty czar bequeathed his three Laff Tissue department staffers a total of $4000. (His wife of forty-eight years and two daughters were left nothing.)

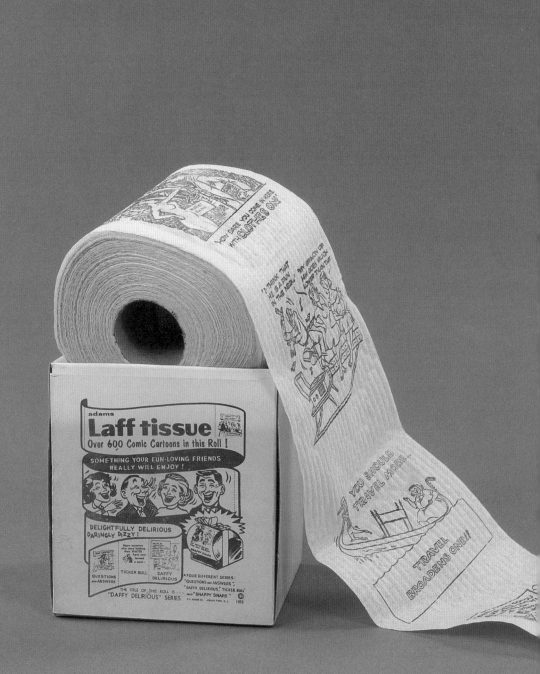

JOKE BOOKS–ASSORTED

DIMENSIONS	4⅞" x 4¾"
ORIGINATOR	Unknown
DATE OF MANUFACTURE	c. 1910s
DESCRIPTION	Sixty-four–page joke books, printed in one color on pulp paper, bound in coated cover stock, printed in three and four colors
MAKER	(Handy Series) Wehman Bros., Park Row, New York City
SLOGAN	"Handy Pocket-Size Books for the Millions"
INSTRUCTIONS	Read and laff (implicit)
UTILITY	Portable joke dispensary
TARGET AUDIENCE	Aspiring verbal humorists
ORIGINAL RETAIL PRICE	10¢
NOTES	"How would you like to be buried in a Hebrew graveyard?" "I'd die first." The lower-Manhattan firm of Wehman Bros. published hundreds, if not thousands, of cheap pulp titles like these from the 1890s through the 1920s and apparently hung on in one form or another through the early 1960s. The tawdry booklets were often retailed in the same catalogs and joke shops that stocked the nation's gags, pranks, and novelties. Prolific if not subtle, the publisher's catalog included: Dutch Jokes; Hebrew Jokes; Irish Jokes; Combination Dutch, Hebrew, Irish Jokes; Coon Jokes; Minstrel Jokes; Tramp Jokes; Farmer Jokes; Rube Jokes; Cowboy Jokes; Clown Jokes; Stage Jokes; Actor Jokes; Ford Jokes; Auto Jokes; Trolly Jokes; After Dinner Jokes; Good Time Jokes; Side Splitting Jokes; Wine Women and Song Jokes; Prize Jokes; New Jokes; Up To Date Jokes; Saucy Jokes; Breezy Jokes; Modern Jokes; Snappy Jokes; Red Hot Jokes; Peachy Jokes; Gingery Jokes; Funny Jokes; Smiles Jokes; Some Jokes; Ha Ha Jokes; and How To Raise Belgian Hares For Pleasure And Profit.

JOKE HYPO DRAWS "BLOOD"
FUNNY PHONY HYPODERMIC
NEEDLE. Appears to draw blood out of
arm, leg, etc. Good joke gag that is
harmless, though it may give the victim
and spectators a real scare.
☐ **2948. Professional Style . . $1.25**

PHONY HYPO

AKA	*Hypo-Squirt, Hypo-Phony, Joke Hypo, Fake Hypo Syringe*
DISPLAY DIMENSIONS	8" x 3 3/4"
INJECTOR DIMENSIONS	3 3/4" x 5/8"
PACKAGE	Polyethylene bag with paper insert, printed in three colors, double—saddle-stitched onto cardboard header with die-punched hole, printed in three colors
ORIGINATOR	Unknown (H. Fishlove & Co. has claimed it)
DATE OF MANUFACTURE	c. 1960s
DESCRIPTION	Three-part molded-plastic syringe packaged with one-inch—square cloth bandage
MAKER	Sosaku Toys (Made in Japan)
SLOGAN	"Drawing or Injecting Blood!"
INSTRUCTIONS	"Fill Injector with red colored water. Draw or press pump slowly, the red water appears or disappears as drawing or injecting blood. Fill black water and draw it. It looks like you have Criminal blood. When Green, you look like creature from another planet."
UTILITY	Creates the illusion of user "Drawing or Injecting Blood"
TARGET AUDIENCE	Children
ORIGINAL RETAIL PRICE	39¢
NOTES	Apparently something of a bottom-of-the-barrel Toyland staple, child-friendly hypodermic needles are given their own ring of hell in the blistering "Toys to Avoid or Discard" section of Edward M. Swartz's 1971 exposé *Toys That Don't Care*. They are roundly dismissed as "psychologically harmful"—and ill-functioning, to boot.

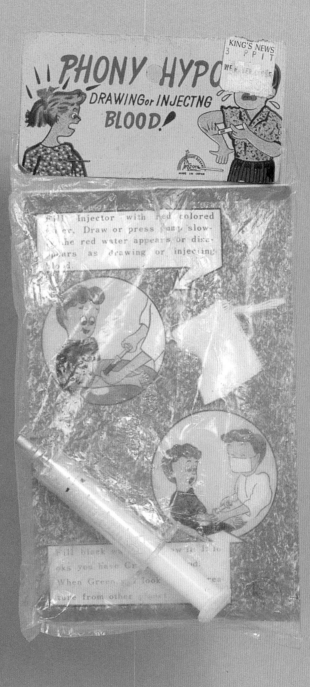

Whoopee Cushion

The Whoopee Cushion or "Poo-Poo" Cushion, as it is sometimes called, is made of rubber. It is inflated in much the same manner as an ordinary rubber balloon and then placed on a chair, couch, seat, etc. When the victim unsuspectingly sits upon the cushion, it gives forth noises that can be better imagined than described.
No. 2953. Whoopee Cushion. Price 25c

WHOOPEE CUSHION

AKA	*Oh-Oh Pillow, The Razzberry, Razzberry Cushion, Razzberry Blower, The Razz, Razz Cushion, Musical Cushion, Poo-Poo Cushion, Poo-Poo Pillow, The Poo Poo Raspberry Cushion, Bronx Cheer, Nature's Rival, Hosslaff Toy, Whoopi Cushion, Flarp*
DIMENSIONS	8⅛" around, with 2" flap
ORIGINATOR	Jem Rubber Co., Toronto, Canada, c. 1930
DATE OF MANUFACTURE	c. 1990s
DESCRIPTION	Inflatable latex balloon with tube closure
MAKER	Anonymous (Made in China)
SLOGAN	"POO, POO"
INSTRUCTIONS	"Do not inflate too heavily"
UTILITY	Mimics sound of prodigious human flatulence when trapped air is forced via external pressure from balloon body outward through tube flap
TARGET AUDIENCE	Pranksters with easy access to the posteriors of scapegoats
ORIGINAL RETAIL PRICE	99¢
NOTES	Astonishingly, the original concept for the pocket Bronx cheer was turned down in 1930 by the creator of itching powder and joke toilet paper, S. S. Adams himself, on the grounds of "poor taste." The simple yet brilliant device was not adopted by Adams until the item became an enormous success with a competing manufacturer. When, in 1994, the Burger King restaurant chain included a polyvinyl rendition of the sixty-year-old novelty with its Kids' Meals program, the company's phone lines were besieged with outraged customers complaining once again of the maligned cushion's "poor taste."

WATER SQUIRT RING

AKA	*The Finger Ring Trick, Novelty Squirt Ring, Diamond Squirt Ring, New Squirt Ring*
DISPLAY DIMENSIONS	6⅝" x 3½"
RING DIMENSIONS	2½" x ¾"
PACKAGE	Polyethylene bag with paper insert, printed in one color, string tied to ring, double—saddle-stitched onto cardboard header, printed in one color
ORIGINATOR	Unknown
DATE OF MANUFACTURE	c. late 1940s
DESCRIPTION	Rubber bulb attached to cast-metal and glass ring
MAKER	Toho (Japan)
SLOGAN	"Water Squirts When Hidden Ball Is Pressed"
INSTRUCTIONS	"Water is ejected from a rubber ball hidden in the hand"
UTILITY	Douses intruder upon one's personal space
TARGET AUDIENCE	Passive-aggressive female pranksters
ORIGINAL RETAIL PRICE	Unknown
NOTES	Joke rings have squirted flustered, unwelcome admirers since time immemorial. This mid—twentieth-century example is a rather meticulously crafted postwar-Japan import with a genuine metal fixture and cut-glass jewel. Within a few years, increasingly available plastic-molding capacities replaced such comparatively extravagant materials, and the product's perceived authenticity suffered greatly, diminishing the effectiveness of the ancient jest.

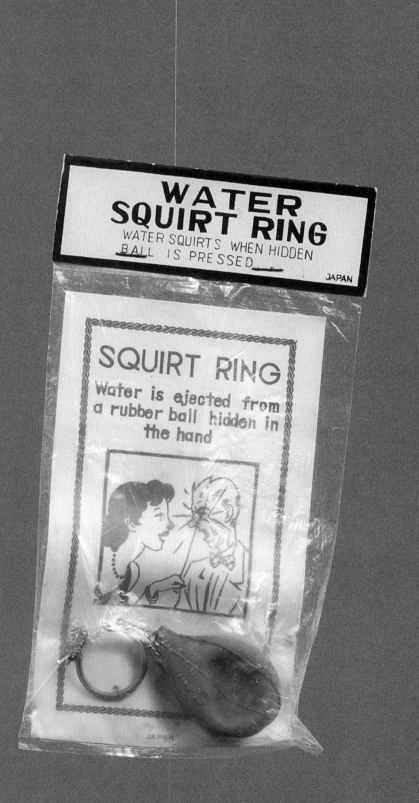

DAZZLE EYES

AKA	*Twinkle Eyes, Winking Eyes, Winky Eyes, Winkin' Eyes, Blinkin' Eyes, Crazy Eyes, Funny Glasses, Zugie Eyes*
DISPLAY CARD DIMENSIONS	7 1/4" x 6 3/8"
GLASSES DIMENSIONS	5" x 1 1/2" x 5 1/8" (unfolded)
PACKAGE	Die-cut cardboard header with die-punched hole, printed in two colors
ORIGINATOR	(Vari-Vue technology) Victor G. Anderson, 1936 (U.S. Patent No. 2,832,593, March 1, 1952); (Dazzle Eyes application) Sol Pritt
PACKAGE DESIGN	George Tagle
DATE OF MANUFACTURE	c. 1950s
DESCRIPTION	Plastic eyeglass frames, two-stage lenticular faux lenses
MAKER	A "Gagmaster" product, manufactured by the Pritt Novelty Co., Inc., New York City; Lens inserts (7L & 7R) manufactured by Vari-Vue™, U.S.A. (U.S. Patent No.s 2,815,310 and 2,832,593)
SLOGAN	"they Wink/they Blink"
INSTRUCTIONS	Apply to bridge of nose and behind helix of outer ear, nod vertically (implicit)
UTILITY	Provides user with the appearance of false, distended orbs in rapid shutter motion
TARGET AUDIENCE	The life of the party (?)
ORIGINAL RETAIL PRICE	Unknown
NOTES	Pictorial Productions, later known as the Vari-Vue company (which coined the term "lenticular"), developed its first multiple-image optical process in the late 1930s and within a decade a New York factory mass produced the novel flickering technology for every imaginable use, from keychains to billboards. Its distinctive yet ephemeral effect can rightly be considered the quintessence of the term "gimmick." The point-of-purchase copy, "Personality Specs.........the life of the party!" is particularly vague, suggesting either that an individual with no personality could acquire one herein for pronto party deployment, or, worse still, that this inanimate object itself has inherently more life and personality than any aspect of the sort of parties the unfortunate consumer could ever hope to attend.

DAZZLE EYES

hey
INK

they
BLINK

ERSONALITY SPECS .... the life of the party!

PSYCHO-CERAMIC

DIMENSIONS	6" x 4½"
ORIGINATOR	Kreiss & Company
DATE OF MANUFACTURE	c. 1960
DESCRIPTION	Cold-glazed ceramic figure, hand-painted in three colors, with plastic string inserts and metal plaque lithographed in one color, attached by metal chain
MAKER	Kreiss & Company (Made in Japan)
SLOGAN	"I'm Not Hard of Hearing, I'm Ignoring You."
INSTRUCTIONS	Display to forestall potential interrupters (implicit)
UTILITY	Office gag gift or decorative personal statement
TARGET AUDIENCE	Knickknack curators not wanting to be interrupted
ORIGINAL RETAIL PRICE	Unknown
NOTES	The aptly named Psycho-Ceramics were introduced in 1958 by Kreiss & Company, a West Coast importer and distributor of cheesy household bric-a-brac of the lowest order. The Psychos enjoyed a brief boom in the gift trade, where they were marketed as the dimensional equivalents of greeting cards. They bear waggish, aggressive, or self-pitying gag messages on an uncompromisingly bizarre cast of cartoon figurines often depicted in mid-psychic trauma or acts of self-mutilation. Other Kreiss series followed suit, featuring funny-message—bearing beatnik, hillbilly, alcoholic, spouse-abused, homeless, or suicidal—yet always essentially cute—characters.

GAG TAGS

AKA *Comic Shipping Tags*

MAILER DIMENSIONS 5" x 7¹/₂"

TAG DIMENSIONS 4³/₄" x 2⁵/₁₆"

PACKAGE Colombian Natural Clasp envelope No. 35, made by the United States Envelope Co., Springfield, Massachusetts, printed in one color, shipped via U.S. Mail

ORIGINATOR U.S. Tag & Ticket, Baltimore, Maryland

DATE OF MANUFACTURE c. 1940s

DESCRIPTION Twenty-four cut-paper tags, die-punched with 11"-long, knotted white string attached at hole, printed in one color

MAKER U.S. Tag & Ticket, Baltimore, Maryland

SLOGAN "All New/All Different/Just For Fun"

INSTRUCTIONS Loop string end onto garment button, wear in public (implicit)

UTILITY Displays humorously aggressive printed message for passive wearer

TARGET AUDIENCE Charles H. Hayes of Worcester, Massachusetts

ORIGINAL RETAIL PRICE $1

NOTES The relatively novel format here cannot conceal the same familiar set of anonymous wisecracks which, with virus-like stealth, infected virtually every twentieth-century printed object with their plebeian rancor. For generations, signs, badges, buttons, postcards, plaques, posters, pennants, labels, decals, cocktail napkins, bubblegum cards, bumper stickers, and T-shirts each quipped a familiar chorus of these workaday one-liners until their utter ubiquity reduced the once-sacred texts to the realm of shopworn shtick.

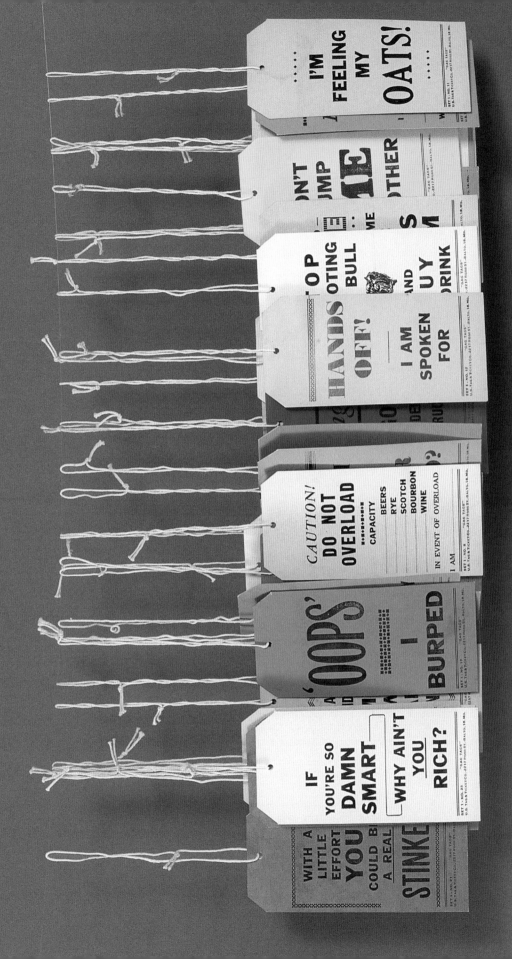

No. 3702—"HOTSY TOTSY" LOVE DOGS. Two small scotty dogs, one black and one white, mounted on licensed Alnico magnet bases. By placing one dog in back of another either dog will be made to dance and whirl, or by placing face to face dogs will draw together. Many other tricks can be performed. A fast selling new item. Mounted twelve pair on display card.

Per Dozen Pair.............................**$1.15**

MAGNETIC SPUNKY DOGS

AKA	*Tricky Dogs, Magnetic Scotty Dogs, Magnetic Live Pups, Magnetic Tricky Pups, Magnetic Fun Loving Pups, Magno-Pups, Novelty Dogs, Spinning Pups, Tricky Pups, Skipper And Scamp, Black And White Scotties, "Hotsy-Totsy" Love Dogs*
DISPLAY DIMENSIONS	3" x 2 1/8"
DOG DIMENSIONS	3/4" x 6/8"
PACKAGE	Polyethylene bag saddle-stitched onto cardboard header, printed in three colors
ORIGINATOR	Irving Fishlove, H. Fishlove & Co., c. 1939
DATE OF MANUFACTURE	c. 1970s
DESCRIPTION	Pair of molded plastic Scottie dog figures with oppositely polarized magnets attached at base
MAKER	Anonymous (Made in China)
SLOGAN	"Lots of Fun!"
INSTRUCTIONS	"They Attract and Repel"
UTILITY	Creates the apparently attention-worthy spectacle of magnetized plastic terriers in kinetic motion
TARGET AUDIENCE	The severely bored
ORIGINAL RETAIL PRICE	Unknown
NOTES	These twin plastic dogs have burrowed so deeply into the collective unconscious of our culture's most marginal consumers and manufacturers that they continue to attract and repel, endlessly—faithfully—decade after decade, without necessity, meaning, point-of-reference, or apparent need for further explanation.

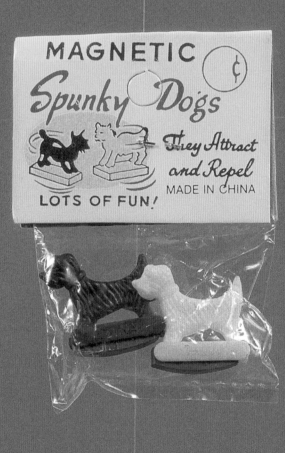

WONDER VOICE THROWER

AKA	*The Ventrillo, The Ventrilo, The Ventro, The Second Voice, The Double Throat*
ENVELOPE DIMENSIONS	2 5/8" x 3 3/4"
OBJECT DIMENSIONS	1" x 5/8"
PACKAGE	Paper envelope, printed in two colors
ORIGINATOR	Unknown
DATE OF MANUFACTURE	c. 1950
DESCRIPTION	Bisected disc composed of wax-paper reed, folded in serrated leather with tin clasp, in paper envelope
MAKER	Anonymous (Japan)
SLOGAN	"BOYS! Learn Ventriloquism and apparently THROW YOUR VOICE!" (Johnson Smith & Co. catalog)
INSTRUCTIONS	"Soak in water until fully saturated, then place on your tongue with the reed nearest the teeth and the finished side of leather upward. Hiss gently at first for a louder sound. Then practice talking and other imitations of birds and animals."
UTILITY	Aids in the ancient art of (apparent) ventriloquism
TARGET AUDIENCE	"BOYS!"
ORIGINAL RETAIL PRICE	10¢
NOTES	The real wonder here is that this essentially useless razor-sharp lozenge was marketed to aspiring junior ventriloquists for so many years without (apparent) legal action.

Wonder VOICE Thrower

Soak in water until fully saturated, then place on your tongue with reed nearest the teeth and the finished side of leather upward. Hiss gently at first, keep on increasing the hiss for a louder sound. Then practice talking and other imitations of birds and animals.

BIRD WHISTLE
PRICE 10¢

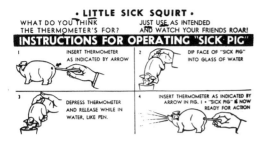

LITTLE SICK SQUIRT

DISPLAY DIMENSIONS	5 1/2" x 5"
SQUIRT DIMENSIONS	2 3/4" x 4 1/2"
PACKAGE	Polypropylene bag, double—saddle-stitched onto cardboard header, printed in one color
ORIGINATOR	Utterly unknown
DATE OF MANUFACTURE	c. 1950s
DESCRIPTION	Two-part, ejection-molded, yellow plastic pig with red-spray highlights, circular-drilled at both ends, containing rubber bulb; clear plastic "thermometer" with red-spray demarcations, attached with transparent tape
MAKER	Absolutely anonymous
SLOGAN	"What Do You Think The Thermometer's For? Just Use As Intended And Watch Your Friends Roar!"
INSTRUCTIONS	"Instructions for Operating 'Sick Pig': 1. Insert thermometer as indicated by arrow 2. Dip face of 'sick pig' into glass of water 3. Depress thermometer and release while in water, like pen 4. Insert thermometer as indicated by arrow in fig 1. 'Sick Pig' is now ready for action!"
UTILITY	Humorist obtains advertised action by pressure, causing toy pig to emit oral effluvia after simulated rectal temperature examination
TARGET AUDIENCE	Bewilderingly unknown
ORIGINAL RETAIL PRICE	Eternally unknown
NOTES	It's tempting to imagine the specific circumstances that must have led to the mass production of such an unfathomable object. Was it one inspired zealot's life-long "million-dollar idea" realized? Could it have been a plastic factory's overrun on stock piggy banks and small clear rods that led to the inevitable brainstorm? How many were made? Where was it sold? Who bought it? Why? Why? Why? Whatever the circumstances, Little Sick Squirt does indeed exist, and that in itself is testimony to the unquenchable spirit of meaningless human achievement.

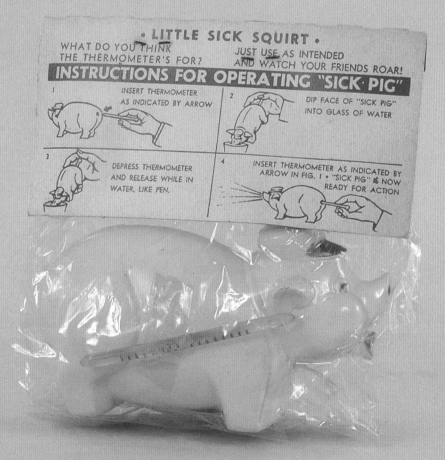

• LITTLE SICK SQUIRT •

WHAT DO YOU THINK
THE THERMOMETER'S FOR?

JUST USE AS INTENDED
AND WATCH YOUR FRIENDS ROAR!

INSTRUCTIONS FOR OPERATING "SICK PIG"

1   INSERT THERMOMETER
    AS INDICATED BY ARROW

2   DIP FACE OF "SICK PIG"
    INTO GLASS OF WATER

3   DEPRESS THERMOMETER
    AND RELEASE WHILE IN
    WATER, LIKE PEN.

4   INSERT THERMOMETER AS INDICATED BY
    ARROW IN FIG. 1 • "SICK PIG" IS NOW
    READY FOR ACTION

Joy Buzzer

No. 1322—JOY BUZZER.
A small buzzer arrangement that is worn in the palm of the hand. When shaking hands the spring is released and produces a "shocking" effect on the victim.
Per Dozen $1.80

THE JOY BUZZER

AKA	*The Tickler, Electric Shocker, Vibrator Hand Shaker, Joke Buzzer, Hand Buzzer, Atomic Buzzer, Hot-Shot Buzzer, Surprise Buzzer, Hand Shaker and Tickler*
VENDING DISPLAY DIMENSIONS	13 1/4" x 12 3/4"
BUZZER DIMENSIONS	1 1/4" around x 1"
ORIGINATOR	Samuel Sorenson Adams; prototype/concept, 1909; final product, 1928 (U.S. Patent No. 1,845,735, November 12, 1931); improved upon and perfected by Joseph (Bud) Adams in subsequent years
DATE OF MANUFACTURE	c. 2004
DESCRIPTION	Circular, cast–zinc-and-tin, mechanical self-winding Joy mechanism with push-button release and attached wire slip ring
MAKER	S. S. Adams Co., Neptune, New Jersey
SLOGAN	"Give Your Friends the Glad Hand with a Razzberry Flavor" (store display, 1930s)
INSTRUCTIONS	"Use the ring as a key to wind it. Wear it as a ring the Buzzer in the palm. It shocks them when they shake hands. It makes them jump if they are ticklish. They will hit the ceiling if they sit on it. Under the sheet it feels like a mouse." (Johnson Smith & Co. ad copy, 1920s)
UTILITY	Used to pinch, shock, and vibrate the exposed palm of the unsuspecting hand shaker
TARGET AUDIENCE	Everyone with fingers and friends
ORIGINAL RETAIL PRICE	Unknown
NOTES	S. S. Adams's masterpiece and the twentieth-century mechanized prank supreme. The shiny, self-winding metal disc from the Jersey shore has been concealed in the ingenuous palms of the century's giants (from Henry Ford to Bugs Bunny) as well as its teeming millions and continues to thrive as the standard in its field as a true American icon of good-natured interpersonal abuse.

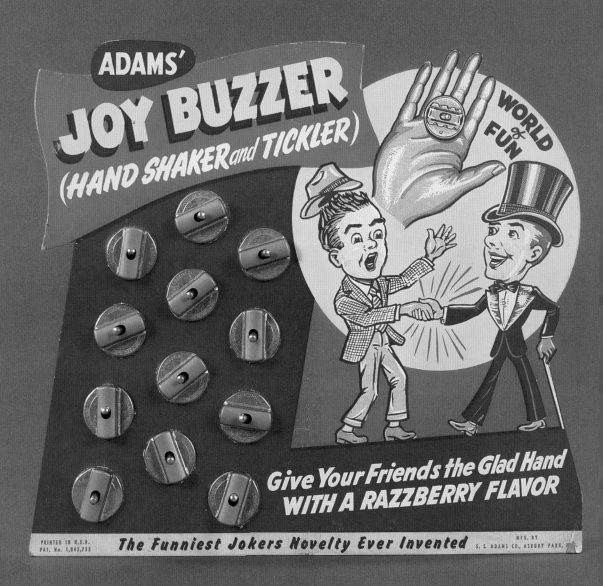

TINY RUBBER MOUSE

This mouse is about 1" long excluding the tail. Made of solid flexible rubber.

Dozen 75c — Gross $8.75

RUBBER MOUSE

AKA	*Solid Rubber Mouse, Hard Rubber Mouse, Tiny Rubber Mouse*
PACKET DIMENSIONS	2³/₁₆" x 3¹/₂"
MOUSE DIMENSIONS	Unknown
PACKAGE	Sealed paper envelope printed in one color
ORIGINATOR	Unknown
DATE OF MANUFACTURE	c. 1960s
DESCRIPTION	A rubber mouse in an envelope
MAKER	Anonymous (Made In Japan)
SLOGAN	"Looks Real"
INSTRUCTIONS	Remove rubber mouse from envelope (implicit)
UTILITY	Realistic rubber mouse, contained in sealed envelope, for unspecified usage
TARGET AUDIENCE	Consumer in need of rubber mouse
ORIGINAL RETAIL PRICE	Unknown
NOTES	Rubber mouse. Apparently looks real.

MADE IN JAPAN

RUBBER MOUSE

LOOKS REAL

RUBBER MOUSE

X-RAY GOGS

AKA	*X-Ray Spex, X-Ray Specs, X-Ray Wonder, Pocket X-Ray, Wonder Tube*
DISPLAY DIMENSIONS	4½" x 6"
GOGS DIMENSIONS	1¾" x 5" (unfolded)
PACKAGE	Polyethylene bag, double–saddle-stitched onto cardboard header with die-punched hole, printed in three colors
ORIGINATOR	Harold Von Braunhut (X-Ray Spex) (U.S. Patent Nos. 3,592,533, 3,711,183 and 4,974,953, June 26, 1969)
DATE OF ORIGIN	c. 1960s
DATE OF MANUFACTURE	c. 1970s
DESCRIPTION	Eyeglass frames with double cardboard inserts containing dyed-red guinea-hen feathers
MAKER	Ming-Shing (#7019) (Made in Hong Kong)
SLOGAN	"Scientific Marvel of the Century"
INSTRUCTIONS	"For the curiously realistic illusion of seeing the bones in your fingers, hold your hand in front of a strong light (about eighteen inches in front of your eyes) fingers spread apart. Tilt your head if vision is blurry."
UTILITY	Provides the wearer the alleged optical effect of seeing the bones in his own fingers
TARGET AUDIENCE	"These screamingly hilarious gogs ensure owners of X-Ray Gogs to be the life of any party."
ORIGINAL RETAIL PRICE	Unknown
NOTES	X-Ray Gogs are an imported knock-off version of the original X-Ray Spex, which in turn were based on the X-Ray Wonder, a monocular tube device that dates to the early years of the twentieth century. Colorful entrepreneur Harold Von Braunhut is also credited with orchestrating such highlights of American marketing savvy as Amazing Live Sea-Monkeys, Crazy Crabs, and Invisible Goldfish, the profits of which apparently helped, in part, to fund such extreme right-wing political groups as the Ku Klux Klan and Aryan Nations.

No. 677 Phony Faucet

A plastic faucet — regular size and natural looking. Attaches to any smooth surface by means of suction cup. Each packed in a clear plastic bubble attached to imprinted instruction card.

No. 677B – EACH IN A BOX

PHONY FAUCET

BOX DIMENSIONS	$3^{15}/_{16}$" x $3^{7}/_{8}$" x 2"
FAUCET DIMENSIONS	4" x $1^{1}/_{2}$" x $3^{3}/_{4}$" (approx.)
PACKAGE	Cardboard box, printed in two colors
ORIGINATOR	H. Fishlove & Co., Chicago (Reg. U.S. Patent Office)
DATE OF ORIGIN	1956
DATE OF MANUFACTURE	1958
DESCRIPTION	Two-part ejection-molded plastic faucet (silver-plated) with applied $1^{3}/_{8}$"-around suction cup
MAKER	H. Fishlove & Co., Chicago
SLOGAN	"Sensational fun gag! Try this on your friends"
INSTRUCTIONS	"Unscrew cup from faucet. Moisten suction cup for better grip. Press on any smooth clean surface. Screw faucet onto the suction cup."
UTILITY	Portable, suction-applied faux faucet for display in "the craziest places"
TARGET AUDIENCE	Aesthetes desiring a non-utilitarian, decorative spigot on a "TV, radio, bookcase, stove, door, fireplace, auto trunk, typewriter, table, bathtub, desk, or piano."
ORIGINAL RETAIL PRICE	Unknown
NOTES	America's reply to Marcel Duchamp's "Fountain" (1917). Both objects function on the incongruous and irrational display of a misplaced plumbing fixture for intended aesthetic effect. Third-generation novelty maker Howard Fishlove (a true pre-Warhol Pop master) went on to market a full-size faux-ceramic urinal before truly one-upping both Duchamp and Andy Warhol by quitting the world of creating useless objects to star in television commercials.

TRICK SMASHED FINGER

AKA	*Bandage Sore Finger Joke, Bloody Finger Trick, Bleeding Finger, Bad Finger, Horrible Finger*
PACKAGE DIMENSIONS	2 1/2" x 3 3/4"
FINGER DIMENSIONS	1 1/2" x 3/4"
PACKAGE	Cardboard header, printed in three colors, saddle-stitched to polyethylene bag
ORIGINATOR	Unknown
DATE OF MANUFACTURE	c. 1950s
DESCRIPTION	Molded-rubber partial digit (second to third metacarpal phalanx) with red spray, gauze bandage saddle-stitched on reverse
MAKER	S.T.K. (Made in Japan)
SLOGAN	"Eloody! [sic] Gory Looking Discolo [sic] Red Swollen Really looks painful"
INSTRUCTIONS	Slip onto unimpaired finger and vocalize (implicit)
UTILITY	Provides user with the appearance of a recently damaged finger
TARGET AUDIENCE	Emotionally deprived children seeking urgent parental concern (and subsequent retribution?)
ORIGINAL RETAIL PRICE	19¢
NOTES	Following the bombings of Hiroshima and Nagasaki, and through the 1970s, low-end rack toys like these were imported from Japan by the millions to America's dime stores. This particular specimen exemplifies the garish header designs that were often swiftly executed by non–English-speaking factory employees, perhaps based on an American jobber's informal product specification.

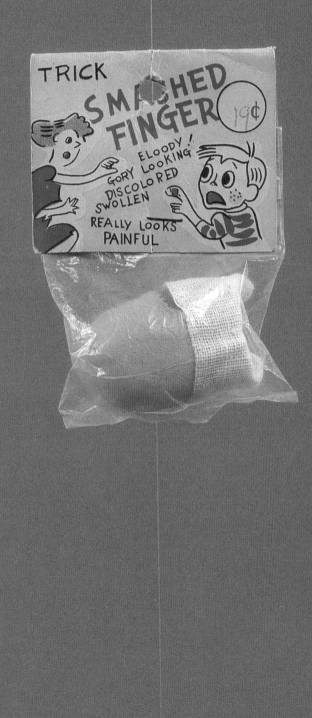

GAGS & JOKES FOR TRAVELLING FOLKS

ENVELOPE DIMENSIONS:	4 1/4" x 6 3/16"
INSERT DIMENSIONS	4 1/4" x 19"
PACKAGE	Paper-board folder with die-cut accordion-fold insert containing eight paper, flexi-coated decalcomania, and cloth sub-inserts, printed in one, two, and four colors
ORIGINATOR	IMPKO (Imprint Art Products, Inc.)
DATE OF MANUFACTURE	c. 1960
DESCRIPTION	Portfolio of paper practical jokes and amusements, framed in postal-mailing cover
MAKER	IMPKO, Hackensack, New Jersey
SLOGAN	"Keep Your Friends Laughing for Hours"
INSTRUCTIONS	"For Fun & Decoration"
UTILITY	"Keep Your Friends Laughing for Hours"
TARGET AUDIENCE	"Travelling Folks"
ORIGINAL RETAIL PRICE	49¢

NOTES   Comparatively extravagant production values were lavished on this handsomely printed gag variety pack. IMPKO specialized in decals and transfers that retailed in hobby, automotive, and specialty shops, also supplying regional roadside attractions with souvenir car-window decorations and pennants. The "Alfred E. Neuman" beatnik decal is an unlicensed usage of a long-standing image whose origin and legal ownership were still open to much debate at the time of manufacture.

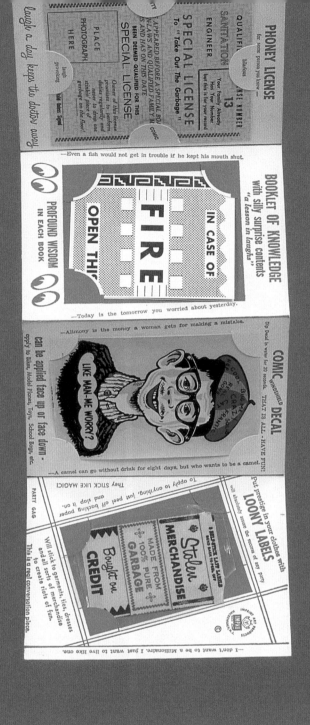

DON'T BE AN ALCHOLIC

BOX DIMENSIONS 6" x 2³/₄" x 1³/₄"

PACKAGE Cardboard gift box with die-cut display insert, each printed in one color

ORIGINATOR Unknown

DATE OF MANUFACTURE c. 1950s

DESCRIPTION Cardboard box containing cardboard insert displaying molded-vinyl mammaries, painted in one color

MAKER Anonymous

SLOGAN "Drink Milk"

INSTRUCTIONS Read box lid, open box, and laff (implicit)

UTILITY Gag gift for alcholics

TARGET AUDIENCE Honored guests attending bachelor parties, "smokers," and other mid-century male-bonding rituals

ORIGINAL RETAIL PRICE Unknown

NOTES Gag gift "Box Gags" can be traced back to the 1920s, pioneered by the Chicago levity factory H. Fishlove & Co. Cheap to manufacture and popular as passive-aggressive party favors, these off-the-cuff novelty sidelines grew to become a literal sub-industry of the business. Early versions included gag-labeled nutshells, hollowed-out books, and other non-standard packaging, humor-enhanced with interior punch lines and attached trinkets. The next generation developed largely as self-mailing joke parcels, popular as long-distance morale boosters for overseas troops during World War II. By the 1950s, the full-blown "Box Gags" were fairly uniform commodities, essentially three-dimensional greeting cards, often aggressive in tone and risqué in content.

"I manufactured Box Gags myself. Box Gags were tremendous. As a matter of fact, I brought Box Gags to Franco, and got them to the point where we made a million Box Gags a year, in the early '60s. Franco's Box Gags were the sensation of the industry. We had the best. We used to make a million Box Gags a year! Now we can't give 'em away for nothing! We had fifty thousand Box Gags I tried to sell to Spencer Gifts three or four years ago. They wouldn't take 'em for nothing!"—Sol Pritt, 2004

Toilet Seat Cover

ROYAL FLUSH

AKA	*Toilet Seat Cover, Oh Johnny*
DIMENSIONS	14" around
ORIGINATOR	Unknown
DATE OF MANUFACTURE	c. 1950s
DESCRIPTION	Double-sided, stitched-cloth, commode-lid adornment, printed in two colors, with dual attached ribbons
MAKER	Unknown
SLOGAN	"Good Bye Cruel World"
INSTRUCTIONS	Enclose seat lid in cloth pocket, secure with ribbon, display with pride (implicit)
UTILITY	Humorous toilet enhancement
TARGET AUDIENCE	Those seeking to aestheticize their guests' privy experiences
ORIGINAL RETAIL PRICE	Unknown
NOTES	The durable scatological/hillbilly humor motif (first widely popularized by the works of vaudevillian and author Charles "Chic" Sale) is coupled here with the comic suicide theme, which emerged significantly in ephemeral objects manufactured during World War II and blossomed to its full black-humor maturity during the Cold War era.

THE WORRY BIRD

AKA	*Worrying George, Worrying Willie, Worrius Relievium, Worry Bird Club Member*
DIMENSIONS	3¾" x 3"
ORIGINATOR	Unknown (open to endless conjecture)
DATE OF MANUFACTURE	c. 1950
DESCRIPTION	Two-part, molded-plastic figure with five hand-applied paint operations, cloaked in dyed rabbit-fur shawl, with spot-glued paper-card insert, printed in one color
MAKER	Unknown
SLOGAN	"Don't be sad,/Don't be blue,/'Cause I'm the bird/Who'll worry <u>for you.</u>"
INSTRUCTIONS	Enshrine, transfer personal anxiety and suffering (implicit)
UTILITY	Totem receptacle for unspecified psychic angst; secular dashboard saint
TARGET AUDIENCE	The worried
ORIGINAL RETAIL PRICE	Unknown
NOTES	Like his cousin Kilroy, the Worry Bird seems to have erupted spontaneously in the collective unconscious of a mid-century America in search of a cartoon character to deify. Claims to the Bird's origin are legion: he was the nose-art mascot for a World War II bomber of the same name; he was created by Tulsa disc jockey Walter Teas in 1950; he was the subject of a song by Leo Robin and Jules Stine in the 1951 RKO musical "Two Tickets to Broadway"; he hailed from "Floogy Boo Manor"; he was created by the influential San Francisco disc jockey Al "Jazzbeaux" Collins; he was the dyslexic mistranslation of the ancient Greek "worry bead" incarnate. What we do know for certain is that he was manufactured in mass quantities starting in the late 1940s in hard plastic, rubber, plaster of Paris, cast metal, and glazed ceramic. There are no known testimonies to his widely held therapeutic efficacy.

KATCHOO POWDER.

A little bit of this powder goes a long way. To create consternation in a gathering of friends a small amount of the powder is simply blown into the room, and immediately everybody begins to sneeze without knowing the cause. A harmless fun producer for practical jokers.

Price 15c.

SNEEZE POWDER

AKA	*Cachoo, Katchoo Powder, Sneezing Powder*
ENVELOPE DIMENSIONS	3 1/2" x 2 1/4"
POWDER DIMENSIONS	Unknown
PACKAGE	Paper tension envelope, printed in one color
ORIGINATOR	Soren Sorenson Adams, 1904
DATE OF MANUFACTURE	c. 1950s
DESCRIPTION	Unidentified powder (likely a dried pepper derivative) in sealed paper envelope
MAKER	Anonymous
SLOGAN	"Harmless Fun!"
INSTRUCTIONS	"To make your victim sneeze simply blow some towards him off the back of your hand. Or sprinkle some on a table. When a magazine is tossed down it will whirl powder into the air."
UTILITY	Induces acute nasal irritation climaxing in repeated spontaneous discharge
TARGET AUDIENCE	Merrymakers with healthy lung capacities, discretionary magazine subscriptions, and accelerated leg responses
ORIGINAL RETAIL PRICE	Unknown
NOTES	In 1904, an ambitious dye-company salesman and professional marksman named Soren Sorenson re-packaged some of the newly imported German coal-tar derivative that had caused contagious sneezing among his co-workers. Sorenson christened the stuff Cachoo in 1906, rechristened himself Samuel Sorenson Adams, and the great American laff industry was born. Today, the S. S. Adams Co. is the leader in its field, but it no longer manufactures Sneezing Powder. "Sneezing Powder contains something that is very injurious," claimed Joseph (Bud) Adams in 1993. "But it's as funny as the devil."

HARMLESS FUN!

To make your victim sneeze, simply blow some toward him, off the back of your hand. Or, sprinkle some on a table. When a magazine is tossed down, it will whirl powder into the air.

KER CHOO!

SNEEZE POWDER

SNAKE NUT CAN
A real looking nut can. Open lid and out pops a snake.
Doz. $2.40 Gr. $27.00

No. A-SNAKE RATTLE CAN
Per Dozen $2.70

SNAKE NUT CAN

AKA	*Snake Surprise Can, Snake in the Can, Snake Can, Jumping Snake Can, Snake Rattle Can*
CAN DIMENSIONS	6¼" x 3"
SNAKE DIMENSIONS	44" x 2"
ORIGINATOR	Contested (Samuel Sorenson Adams and Sam Oumano both lay claim)
DATE OF MANUFACTURE	c. 1930s
DESCRIPTION	Metal faux-snack can with screw-top lid, spray-painted in one color with affixed die-cut label, printed in one color; contains coiled-metal spring "snake" with stitched-fabric covering, hand-painted in three colors, and attached styrofoam head, hand-painted in two colors with embedded plastic-doll eyes and felt fringe lashes attached
MAKER	S. S. Adams Company, Neptune, New Jersey
SLOGAN	"A Real Nutty Surprise"
INSTRUCTIONS	Leave as snack bait for intended victim (implicit)
UTILITY	Snare loaded to startle unwary peanut-brittle–seeking boosters
TARGET AUDIENCE	Madcaps with peanut-brittle–seeking boosters in their lives
ORIGINAL RETAIL PRICE	50¢
NOTES	Over the years, springy serpents of all lengths have leapt out of every conceivable decoy nest, from kinetoscopes to flashlights. While this vintage S. S. Adams Co. example was manufactured during the Depression years, the company later achieved something approaching industry standardization with its "Fancy Salted Mixed Nuts" treatment, which dates back a half-century and still remains in continuous production. Variants, however, may still be observed: Adams continues to market updated versions with its signature headless snakes coiled tightly inside yogurt cups and stacked-potato-chip containers. "Adams had the best snake and the best can. Of all the nut cans, his were the best."—Sol Pritt, 2004

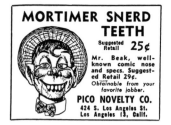

MORTIMER SNERD TEETH

AKA	*Goofy Teeth, Rube Teeth, Comic Buck Teeth, Simple Simon Teeth, Buck Teeth U.S.A.*
DISPLAY DIMENSIONS	3¹/₂" x 5¹/₂"
TEETH DIMENSIONS	1¹/₄" x 1³/₄"
PACKAGE	Cardboard, printed in two colors, with double–saddle-stitched cellophane bag
ORIGINATOR	Unknown
DATE OF MANUFACTURE	c. 1950s
DESCRIPTION	Pink wax upper-dental plate with embedded plastic mis-matched central and lateral incisors
MAKER	Pico Novelty Co., Los Angeles, California
SLOGAN	"Fun For Everyone!"
INSTRUCTIONS	"Directions—Hold red dental wax over flame (gas or match) or steam until pliable. Fold wax and place in groove at top of teeth. Place in mouth, bite firmly hold in place for one minute. TEETH NOW FIT WHENEVER YOU DESIRE TO WEAR THEM"
UTILITY	Portable discretionary simulated overbite in the beloved manner of Edgar Bergen's ventriloquist figure
TARGET AUDIENCE	"For Men • Women • Kiddies"
ORIGINAL RETAIL PRICE	25¢
NOTES	A rare Hollywood-character–endorsed novelty. The low profit margins on these cheaply retailed items discouraged the feasibility of any product already burdened with licensing fees. Other 1950s examples include "Snoz," a Jimmy Durante-advertised rubber nose, and "Groucho Goggles," the moustache, big nose, and glasses combo with an added plastic-cigar attachment sold under the direct authorization of Mr. Arthur Marx himself.

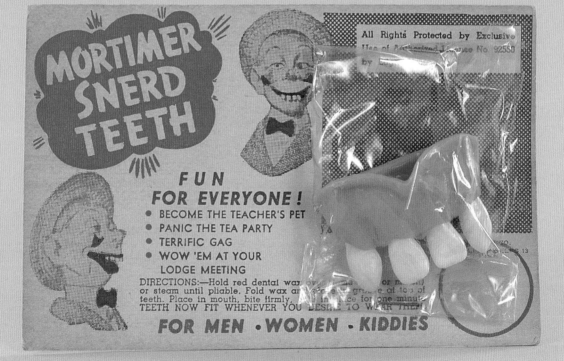

LONG ASHES

AKA	*Gee Whiz Fake Cigarette Ashes, Fake Cigar & Cig. Butts*
BOX DIMENSIONS	5¹⁄₂" x 2" x 4¹⁄₄"
ASH DIMENSIONS	3³⁄₄" x ¹⁄₈"
PACKAGE	Die-cut cardboard box, printed in four colors
ORIGINATOR	Unknown
DATE OF MANUFACTURE	c. 1950
DESCRIPTION	2¹⁄₄" x ¹⁄₈"-around, printed, cloth-covered spring applied to 1¹⁄₂"-long machine-twisted wire
MAKER	Anonymous (Stock #17463, Made in Japan)
SLOGAN	"A Terrific Joke!"
INSTRUCTIONS	"Fool your friends"
UTILITY	Cigar prosthesis of excessive length
TARGET AUDIENCE	Cigar users with friends
ORIGINAL RETAIL PRICE	Unknown
NOTES	Packed twelve dozen to a display box, these were evidently expected to really fly off the retail counters. Exactly what the "terrific joke" inherent in an extended cigar ash might be is any historian's guess.

COMIC FUN CERTIFICATE –
ANCIENT ORDER OF BELCHERS

AKA   *Gag License, Joke Certificate, Fun Certificate*

DIMENSIONS   8" x 10½"
ORIGINATOR   Unknown
DATE OF MANUFACTURE   c. 1936
DESCRIPTION   Paper, printed in two colors
MAKER   Magnotrix Novelty Corp., New York, New York
SLOGAN   "Blurp/Ump/Burp"

INSTRUCTIONS   Fill out ceremonial form with intended's name and present or display (implicit)
UTILITY   Template-printed offense for individual customization and presentation
TARGET AUDIENCE   Unsympathetic acquaintance of acid-reflux–syndrome sufferer
ORIGINAL RETAIL PRICE   5¢

NOTES   Yet another delineation of the pre-manufactured personal affront whose unsavory history spans the "penny dreadful" insult valentines of the Civil War era to the Garbage Pail Kids stickers of the recent past, leaving a smoking trail of permanently damaged psyches in its wake. These ersatz documents were also produced as wall plaques, postcards, or "Exhibit" cards, dispensed in penny-arcade machines and as deluxe versions printed on parchment, apparently created for proud, permanent home display.

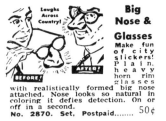

BEAGLE PUSS

AKA *Big Nose & Glasses, The Beak, Mr. Beak, Mr. Schnozz, Schnozola, 4-Piece Schnozola, Groucho Goggles, Groucho Specs, Snoopy Puss, Mustachio Mr. Beak, Gay Nineties Specs, Specs Tash N' Nose, Fuzzy Nose Glasses, Disguise Set, The Hawkshaw Mask or Terrible Pete*

DISPLAY DIMENSIONS 7" x 5¼"

PUSS DIMENSIONS 4½" x 5¾" (unfolded)

PACKAGE Die-cut cardboard header with die-punched hole, printed in two colors

ORIGINATOR Unknown/disputed

DATE OF MANUFACTURE c. 1970s

DESCRIPTION Plastic eyeglass frames with saddle-stitched, molded-rubber nose and adhesive-tipped, rabbit-fur moustache and eyebrow pieces

MAKER Franco-American Novelty Co., Glendale, New York

SLOGAN "The World's Funniest Disguise"

INSTRUCTIONS Apply to bridge of nose and behind helix of outer ear (implicit)

UTILITY Provides user with the mocking appearance of "city slicker" (i.e., Jewish intellectual)

TARGET AUDIENCE Consumers who demand the world's funniest disguise

ORIGINAL RETAIL PRICE Unknown

NOTES "My brother invented them. They were beautifully made. You walked in a room and it looked like you had a real big nose. You couldn't tell the difference. Now it's a quickie thing."—Louis St. Pierre, proprietor, Hollywood Magic Shop, *The Wall Street Journal,* 1990

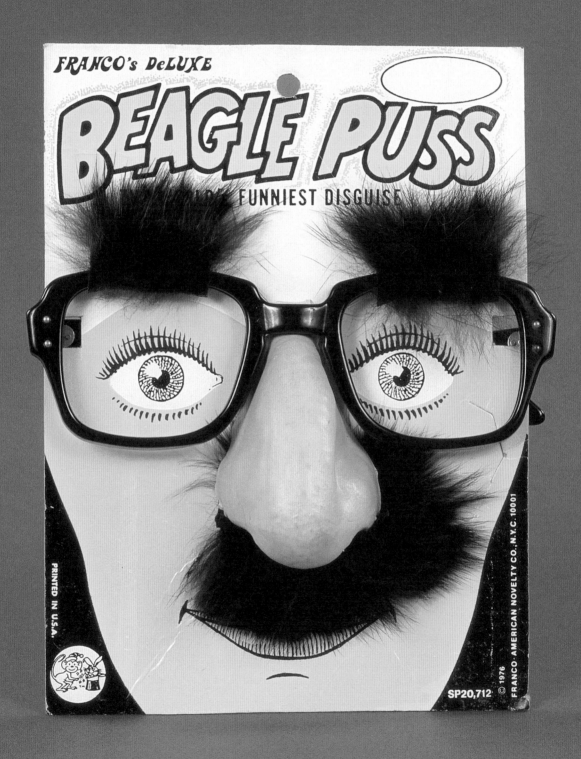

TANTALIZING TEASPOON

AKA	*Joke Teaspoon, No Sip Teaspoon*
BOX DIMENSIONS	2" x 6" x 1$^1/_{16}$"
SPOON DIMENSIONS	5$^3/_4$"
PACKAGE	Cardboard box, printed in one color
ORIGINATOR	Unknown
DATE OF MANUFACTURE	c. 1940s
DESCRIPTION	Metal spoon with clear plastic cap attached to bowl
MAKER	Franco, New York (No. 239) (Franco-American Novelty Co., Glendale, New York)
SLOGAN	"It is a Real Laugh Maker"
INSTRUCTIONS	"The invisible material applied to the bowl of this spoon, makes it impossible to hold any food."
UTILITY	Inoperative silverware for Mister Wise-Guy's table setting
TARGET AUDIENCE	Hosts of ill-favored dining companions
ORIGINAL RETAIL PRICE	Unknown
NOTES	Presumably to be offered with a gentle repast of Comic Hot Dogs, Rubber Buns, Stone Chocolates, and Awful Tasting Cola. A mid-century monkeyshine marketed by the Franco-American Novelty Co., which can trace its history back to 1909 and to a Broadway joke dispensary tended by the legendary Sam Oumano. The family-run establishment is still a force in the laff industry; today, an interested party can procure nearly everything from Super Size Jumbo Afros to Kitty Crap (wholesale only).

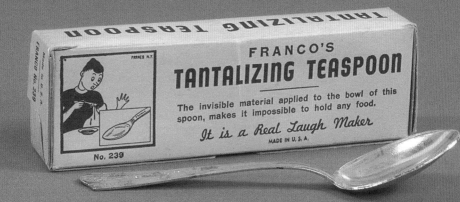

COMIC PLAQUES
Funny and witty slogans and sayings on cardboard plaques that will make people laugh and snicker wherever shown.

Per Hundred $3.50

COMIC PLAQUE

AKA	*Bar Room Plaque, Gag Plaque, Fun Signs, Smart-Remark Plaques, Wacky Plaks*
DIMENSIONS	9" x 11¾"
ORIGINATOR	Unknown (although there are claims to certain texts by David Gilbert of Milbit Mfg.)
DATE OF MANUFACTURE	c. 1950s
DESCRIPTION	Varnished-pine rectangle shingle with one-color silk-screen spray and twin, 1/8"-diameter drilled holes
MAKER	Anonymous
SLOGAN	"Danger/Men Drinking"
INSTRUCTIONS	Display on wall, bask in admiration (implicit)
UTILITY	Humorous but no-nonsense directive, designed for calculated effect and permanency
TARGET AUDIENCE	Home bartenders and homebound drinkers
ORIGINAL RETAIL PRICE	Unknown
NOTES	The affluence of post-war America afforded yet another venue for the sacred gag texts that had migrated throughout the twentieth century between all printed media: the walls of the "bachelor pad" and the private bars and "rumpus rooms" of suburbia. These chapels of male bonding thrived in the 1950s and '60s, providing an ideal breeding ground for the fruits of the cheap-laffs industry as well as other, more expensive toys specifically designed for and marketed to the new consumer base of jocular pseudo-alcoholics.

The Funny Chatterbox

Just Pull The Tape And It Talks To You

This queer contraption is certainly the very latest in the novelty line. It is a sort of a portable phonograph made in the shape of a round metal box with a piece of tape, made of a special material about a yard long. Pull the tape from left to right and the box will say in a loud understandable voice: "HELLO SWEETHEART." Or another box will say: "COME UP AND SEE ME SOME TIME." Another box will say: "SAY, DO YOU WANNA BUY A DUCK?" Pull the tape back again and it is all set to talk to you or your friends again as often as you wish. It is entertaining and amusing, and an entirely new fun maker. The box is well made of metal and presents a very attractive appearance. Be sure to specify which of the three sayings you want. Send a quarter in stamps or silver and let Chatterbox speak for itself.

No. 2965. THE FUNNY CHATTERBOX. Price Postpaid.................. **25c**

"HELLO SWEETHEART! I'M THE TALKING WOLF!"

AKA	*The Funny Chatterbox*
BOX DIMENSIONS	6" x 5¼"
WOLF DIMENSIONS	3" x 2½" x 2"
PACKAGE	Cardboard box with die-cut silhouette display window, printed in two colors
ORIGINATOR	Unknown (Talking-ribbon technology, Thomas A. Edison c. 1900s)
DATE OF MANUFACTURE	c. 1940s
DESCRIPTION	Two-part, molded-plastic wolf bust with cardboard baseplate and attached plastic ribbon
MAKER	Noma Electric Corporation (Cat. No. 755), New York 11, N.Y.
SLOGAN	"I'm A Friendly Wolf/A Fellow Really Fine/For Absolute Proof—Listen To My Line!"
INSTRUCTIONS	"To make me talk, start at top and draw thumbnail along ridges of my plastic ribbon. For best results hold me lightly and draw tape gently"
UTILITY	Semi-mechanical attention-seeking proxy
TARGET AUDIENCE	Bashful sexual predators
ORIGINAL RETAIL PRICE	Unknown
NOTES	During the material shortages of World War II, the Noma Electric Corporation, renowned as a premier American manufacturer of Christmas-tree lights, shifted its efforts to what went *under* the tree and undertook its first lines of dolls, toys, and assorted novelties. The crude sound technology that gives this wicked wolf his sweet-talking pickup line was adapted from an original Edison patent from the early 1900s, and first entered the joke shop as a talking box minus the lupine encasement.

MAGIC SNAKES

AKA | *Mysterious Serpent's Eggs, Pharaoh's Snakes, Eggs Of Pharaoh's Serpents, Snakes In The Grass, Snake In Hat, Snake Loads, Snake Volcanoes, Growing Snake Eggs, Trick Snakes, Barrel Snakes, Glo Worms, Sooner Pills*

VENDING DISPLAY DIMENSIONS | $12\frac{1}{2}$" x 7"
PACKET DIMENSIONS | $2\frac{1}{4}$" x $2\frac{1}{8}$"
PACKAGE | Paper envelope, printed in one color
ORIGINATOR | Unknown
DATE OF MANUFACTURE | c. 1960s
DESCRIPTION | Paper envelope containing dried pellets of mercuric thiocyanate $Hg(CNS)_2$, attached to cardboard vending display with die-punched hole and grommet, saddle-stitched into polyethylene bag
MAKER | Anonymous (I.D. #T/10-15-1)
SLOGAN | "Guaranteed Not to Contain Poisonous Mercury"

INSTRUCTIONS | "Light at End of Pellet, will form into a large Snake ·······Will Not Bite/'DO NOT PUT IN MOUTH'"
UTILITY | When ignited, mercuric thiocyanate pellet burns rapidly, leaving a coiled, black serpentine ash in its wake
TARGET AUDIENCE | Those presumably under adult supervision
ORIGINAL RETAIL PRICE | Unknown

NOTES | The unholy crossroad where cheap novelty, low-end magic trick, and illicit firework intersect. These noxious capsules were at one time piously marketed under the name "Pharaoh's Serpents," in reference to several incidents of serpentine transformation in *Exodus*. They were also offered up during the Depression in conjunction with a class of scatological novelties mysteriously referred to as "Sooners"—metal figures in squatting positions, as well as with small ceramic commodes.

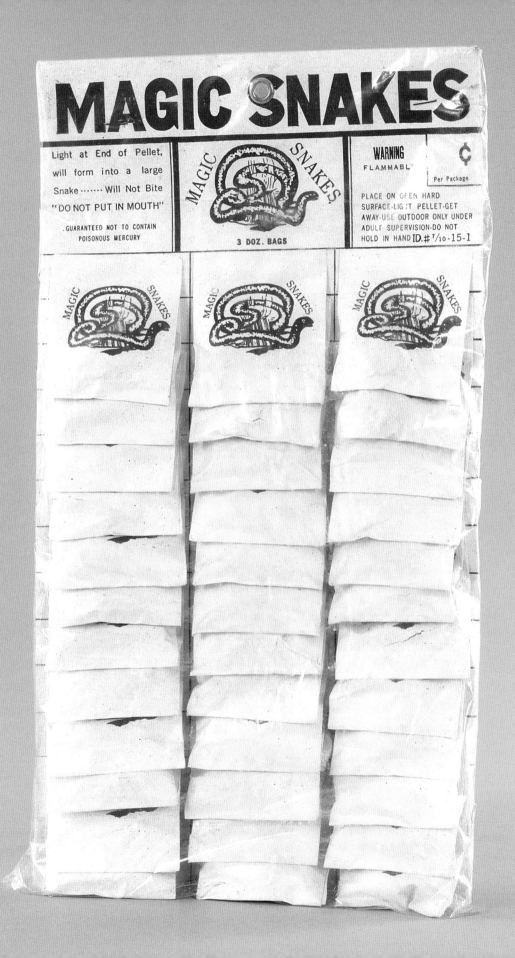

DRY DAN THE DRINKING MAN

AKA	*Drinking Bird, Ever Drinking Bird, Happy Bird, Happy Drinking Bird, Goofy Drinking Bird, Amazing Drinking Bird, Thirsty Bird, Dippy Bird, Dipee Bird, Dunking Bird, Thermodynamic Bird, The Twinkle Bird, Ever Drinking Perpetual Motion Goofy Bobbing Bird, Ever Drinking Penguin, The Golden Bird, The Orange Bird, The Drinking Duck, Magic Dunking Duck, Tic Toc Ever Drinking Bird, Dippy-Dilly, Daffy-Dilly, The Drinking Giraffe*
BOX DIMENSIONS	2" x 6½" x 2"
MAN DIMENSIONS	7" x 1¾"
PACKAGE	Cardboard box, printed in four colors
ORIGINATOR	Miles V. Sullivan, 1946 (U.S. Patent No. 240,002,243, August 6, 1945)
DATE OF MANUFACTURE	c. 1960s
DESCRIPTION	Model of male alcoholic composed of two-part, molded-plastic legs and feet base, enclosed glass beaker tube with twin bulbs at each end containing red fluid (likely methylene chloride or diethyl ether), which rests on die-punched recesses in legs via attached aluminum pivot. Tube is decorated with vinyl coat and plastic clasp, styrofoam head and nose with attached, die-cut vinyl-transfer mouth and eyes, printed in one color. Plastic hat and inserted lock of human hair.
MAKER	Anonymous ("Made in Taiwan Republic of China")
SLOGAN	"Once He Starts Drinking He Won't Stop"
INSTRUCTIONS	"1. Insert the Pivot into the openings at the top of the two legs as per photo [sic] and make the MAN move to and fro freely. 2. Fill a glass with cold water, height of glass should be a little lower than that of the legs. 3. Put the head into the water and make it get wet completely and place the MAN near the glass, then the MAN begin [sic] drinking water HIMSELF."
UTILITY	"Great Fun for Everyone"
TARGET AUDIENCE	Everyone
ORIGINAL RETAIL PRICE	Unknown
NOTES	A rare non-fowl incarnation of the world's most persistent physics/chemistry novelty, perhaps geared to the niche market of the bored yet scientifically inclined co-dependant.

Dog Floor Mess

Poor Fido! From the looks of the mess on carpet, he wasn't let out last night. Dog gets the blame until they start to clean it up—and then they discover what an amazingly real imitation it is. Work it over and over again. The victim might buy it from you for $1.00 to pull on someone else.

No. 2999. Price **20c**

DELUXE DOGGIE DIRT

AKA *Dog Gonnit, Doggonit Floor Novelty, Dog Dun It, Doggie Doo, Dog Floor Mess, Bad Dog, Jumbo Dog Turd, Dog Drops, Plop, Mucky Pup, Kilroy Was Here*

DIMENSIONS 4" x 4³/₄" (depending on orientation)

ORIGINATOR Unknown/disputed (Sam Oumano has been credited, but verification is lacking)

DATE OF MANUFACTURE c. 1990s

DESCRIPTION Realistically molded papier-mâché sham dropping with one-color paint coat

MAKER Anonymous, distributed by Franco-American Novelty Co., New York (No. 0746)

SLOGAN "Best Quality" (Catalog #11, 1999)

INSTRUCTIONS Display upon appropriate venue (implicit)

UTILITY Achieves highly realistic presentation of abandoned dog feces

TARGET AUDIENCE Conspirators with dog-sensitive victims

ORIGINAL RETAIL PRICE Unknown

NOTES "Who created fake dog doo? I don't know who. How far do dogs go back? When was the dog invented?"—Joseph (Bud) Adams, President of the S. S. Adams Co., 1993

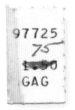

Acknowledgements:

For interviews, assistance, loans, and support, we wish to thank: the late
Joseph (Bud) Adams; Jordan Bochanis; Megan Montague Cash; Brian Dewan;
Erick Erickson; Amy Gray; George Horner; Ben Katchor; John Keene; John
Kelly; *marvinglass.com*; Sol Pritt; Graham Putnam; William V. Rauscher;
Rose Shamus; Rita Simon; Stan and Mardi Timm; and Domenique Zuber.
Special thanks to Chris Adams, of the S. S. Adams Company, for graciously
allowing a tour of the factory and lending archival materials.

Guilty Parties:

Mark Newgarden is a cartoonist, writer, and sometime novelty-smith living in
Brooklyn, New York. He created the Garbage Pail Kids, among other warped
and weird gimmicks. His work has appeared in the Smithsonian Institution
and the Brooklyn Museum of Art, as well as in publications ranging from
RAW to *The New York Times*. His recent projects include writing and direct-
ing the B. Happy cartoon series for *cartoonnetwork.com*. A collection of his
work, *We All Die Alone*, will be published in 2005. (www.laffpix.com)

PictureBox, Inc. is a New York-based visual-content studio and publishing
house composed of Peter Buchanan-Smith and Dan Nadel. Previous projects
include *Speck* and *Fresh Dialogue Four*. Most recently, PictureBox published
The Wilco Book. The studio also continues to produce the ongoing annual
book of pictures and prose *The Ganzfeld*, and is currently at work on a history
of comics to be published in 2005. (www.pictureboxinc.com)

Michael Schmelling's photographs have appeared in numerous national and
international publications. A book of his photographs from El Paso, Texas,
Shut Up Truth, was published in 2002. (www.michaelschmelling.com)